Disclaimer

Although the author and publisher have made every effort to ensure that the information in this book was correct at press time, the author and publisher do not assume, and hereby disclaim, any liability to any party for any loss, damage, or disruption caused by errors or omissions, whether such errors or omissions result from negligence, accident, or any other cause.

Information contained in this book is intended as an educational aid only. Information is not intended as medical advice for individual conditions or treatment, and is not a substitute for a medical examination, nor does it replace the need for services provided by medical professionals.

All content contained in this publication is for information purposes only. You will not hold Solutions from Science or the author responsible if any harm comes to you as a result of information contained in this guide. All commentary is protected by free speech.

Dedication

This book is dedicated to Abigail Adams, wife of John Adams, one of our Founding Fathers.

Abigail was the daughter of a parson and was taught to read and write because those skills were necessary for reading the Bible and doing household accounts. However, all of her life she pursued self-education, and she became one of the best read and most literate women in the colonies and the new United States. She was easily the equal of most men in her political astuteness and acumen. Intelligent, compassionate, sensible, obstinate, hard-working, proud, inventive, frugal, and resourceful, she was filled with a sense of duty to the country whose birth pangs thundered all around her. She bore seven children (losing two of them in childhood), survived several epidemics, and ran a farm and several households virtually single-handed. She was separated from the man she loved for years at a time as he attended to the business of a fledgling country, but she rarely complained. She never gave up, although she was often tired, ill and in great fear.

In a letter dated June 5, 1775 to John (who was in Philadelphia as Massachusetts's delegate to the Continental Congress), she asked:

> *I have a request to make of you.... It is, that you would send out Mr. Bass, and purchase me a bundle of pins and put them in your trunk for me. The cry for pins is so great that what I used to buy for seven shillings and sixpence are now twenty shillings, and not to be had for that.*

Imported goods were nowhere to be found in the new country, and inflation sent costs through the roof. No one would take paper money, which devalued if they had it for more than two weeks. When John was in France for the second time in 1780, he sent her small presents of laces, ribbons, tea, glassware and handkerchiefs—which she promptly sold to keep their family afloat. The handkerchiefs were a big hit, and Abigail began to put in specific requests for silk ones because they commanded double the price of linen ones, though they didn't cost any more in Europe. She ordered cloth by the yard, and other items such as brushes and bowls, and started her own import business. Eventually, John suggested she just write straight to the merchants themselves. She did, and sold the goods herself or through others. In this way the family made it through a severe drought, crushing taxes, and high prices.

Abigail wouldn't recognize the United States today, but she would recognize the spirit of individuals who care about their country and who, without flinching, take the responsibility for themselves and their family fully onto themselves. Abigail Adams was a Founding Mother as surely as her husband, John, was a Founding Father. She should also be the prepper's patron saint. When you tire and want to give up, remember Abigail: *"Great difficulties may be surmounted by patience and perseverance."*

The Ant and the Turkey

A Modern Fable

One beautiful summer day a Turkey was having a party to celebrate Lindsey Lohan being let out of jail. He and all his turkey friends were singing and gobbling and flapping around on the hill where they lived. The music was loud and lively, and there was plenty of beer and barbeque for everyone. They were having a wonderful time. Every few hours a turkey flew down the hill to get more beer and chips from the convenience store, and he always returned with more turkeys who wanted to party.

As he was kicking back on his deck with a cold brew in his hand, the Turkey watched an Ant who lived on the hill next to him who was busy gathering and storing grain, chopping wood for his fireplace, and stocking up on medicine. He was so amazed he stopped partying for a minute and went to talk to the Ant.

"Why are you working so hard?" he asked the Ant. "It's summer and Lindsey is free! Come on over and party with us. Have a beer and chill out a little. Seriously, you look like you could use a vacation."

"Winter is coming. I am worried about my family and I want them to be able to live through it," said the Ant, who really was very tired and could have used a vacation, but he had spent his money on an electric distiller, a Crisis Cooker, and food. "I am storing up food, fuel, and medicine for the winter. I think you should do the same."

"Dude, don't harsh my mellow," said the Turkey. "Winter is a long way off. There is plenty of food, and even if there isn't, the government promised to bring us some anyway."

As the Turkey turned away to return to his party, he said, "You know, Ant, you are really no fun at all. You're a serious downer and you're depressing the whole neighborhood."

The Ant sighed. He felt sad for the turkey and his friends. He could hear them laughing at him even across the valley, but he kept on sealing up his food.

Then one day the music and lights over on the Turkey's hill went out. Even worse, there was no beer or barbeque available to be bought for any amount of money (even if they'd had any, which they didn't, because it had become useless paper overnight).

Within three days the Turkey and his friends were starving, thirsty, and cold, and they began to eye the Ant's hill with desperation. The turkeys were very angry because it didn't look like the government was going to be giving them food or fuel after all. They charged over to the Ant's hill, intending to take his food and wood so they would be able to live. But the Ant had a big mean dog and his house was strong, and his family knew how to defend it.

"You danced and sang all last summer," shouted the Ant in disgust. "You called me names and laughed at me because I wouldn't party with you. Now you will have to take care of yourselves." Then he let out his big mean dog and the turkeys retreated in disarray.

In the following days, the turkey's hill grew very quiet. The Ant and his family lived through the winter. It wasn't fun and the Ant was still very tired. He really, really did need a vacation—a long one where he sipped margaritas on a lovely beach at sunset and watched the waves roll in. But it was enough that he and his family were warm, fed, and had enough water to drink.

Moral: Failing to plan is planning to fail.
~ Benjamin Franklin ~

Table of Contents

INTRODUCTION

Hope for the best, but plan for the worst.

Why Plan for the Worst?

Preparing to survive the worst-case catastrophe requires courage, endurance, and dedicated long-term planning. It means accepting that the worst case scenario is possible, understanding how devastating it would be, and appreciating how quickly it could happen.

Most of us deny that the possibility of a worst-case scenario even exists and continue to lead our busy, comfortable lives. No one wants to think about what would happen to us and our loved ones if the world as we know it collapsed around us. But if you are reading this, you are different.

About 98% of Americans live in an urban environment. We are totally dependent on systems we do not understand and without which we are helpless. Clean water flows out of the tap with a flip of our wrist. Food comes from the supermarket in shrink-wrapped packages and attractively printed microwavable boxes from the store. The car starts with the turn of a key, and we can go anywhere we want at any time.

We may grumble that gas costs too much, but it is always there. We flip a switch and the lights turn on. We turn the thermostat up or down at will to maintain our comfort levels. The police and justice system are there to control the worst elements of our society. Medical and dental care can be accessed one way or the other. We know that we can find any type of information we want instantly, through a nearly infinite variety of sources.

We truly live blessed lives. But the flip side of that blessing is a curse. The reality is that, if our life-support systems stop without warning, then our lives may hinge on the decisions we make and the actions we take in the <u>next 72 hours,</u> and how well we have prepared for everything <u>after 72 hours</u>.

Those who choose to prepare live by the motto: *"Hope for the best, but plan for the worst."* It is NOT wrong to hope for the best, but it IS reckless in these unstable times to ONLY hope for the best and take no steps to prepare for the worst. "Preppers" are often accused of being cynical, of giving up, or of choosing to live in a state of perpetual misery and fear. However, the reverse is true.

Preparing allows you to fully live and hope in the present because you know that the initial onslaught of the worst will not stun you into paralysis or send you spiraling into panic—either of which could imperil your life and the lives of your family. Preparing gives you a buffer zone in which you can make better, life-saving decisions as the future you are now facing emerges.

As a prepper, you will quickly learn that bringing the subject up often results in scorn and criticism being heaped upon you by neighbors, co-workers, friends and even your family. They think you are foolish for packing a life raft for your voyage on the *Titanic*. The whole idea is nonsense! You're a doomsayer! Everyone knows that the United States, just like the *Titanic*, is unsinkable!

But if the worst happens, these people (as kind and decent as they are) will spend the first hours and days of a catastrophe scrambling to just make sense of the chaos, much less deal with it. They will waste precious time in long lines at the gas station trying to get the last available gas or trying to sweep anything—ANYTHING—left on the shelves of the supermarket into their carts. They will be in a panic trying to track down their scattered family, or desperately trying to get the last available cash from the ATM. They will be critically behind the survival curve from the start

Those who have studied survivors have found that 10% of people panic, endangering themselves and others; 80% wait for someone to tell them what to do or simply freeze; and 10% take some kind of action. The action may or may not save their lives, but they didn't sit there impassively waiting for death. Preparing means that you can avoid a panic state and not be stunned into immobility awaiting instructions. It will allow you to move swiftly to assemble your family and assess the situation as calmly as you can under the terrifying circumstances. Planning will give you the space and time to make the best decisions you can, which might save you and your family's lives.

No one can see over the horizon or around corners, but (especially if you have people and animals dependent on you), you have the RESPONSIBILITY to try to anticipate as best you can. If you are ready to take that responsibility, this guide is your blueprint to doing it quickly, efficiently, and with the least waste of scarce resources.

The Three Steps to Survival

A journey of a thousand miles starts with a single step.
~Lao Tzu, Chinese philosopher~

The First Step

You can't prepare physically until you have prepared mentally. You have to internalize that a worst-case scenario could happen. This is not easy to do when the world appears to be ticking along, more or less smoothly around you, and everyone else seems content to continue operating normally, oblivious to the dangers of a world on edge. However, you must internalize the idea that one day you may wake up in the "Old World" and go to bed in a "New World", and that the "New World" might be indescribably grim for an unknown amount of time.

The Second Step

If you decide to prepare, you must make a commitment to yourself to devote the time and resources necessary to the project. Make no mistake about it—prepping is a huge undertaking. The level of preparation you choose will depend on what you set as your personal goal: three days to a week (3-5-7 track); several months or even years with limited, rationed, expensive or unavailable services and goods (FEND track); or living "Off The Grid" (OTG track) altogether. Preparing for the first track—a short-term recoverable emergency—is easy, but preparing for the FEND and OTG tracks are not. They take planning, commitment, budgeting of resources, time and a lot of work.

You must carefully consider your financial resources and the time you can reasonably bring to bear on the project given your other responsibilities. Unless you are blessed with unlimited free time and remarkable financial resources, this project will take quite a while and will absolutely strain a tight budget. For most of us, making this commitment will mean prioritizing, making real sacrifices, and creatively seeking out the most inexpensive means of achieving our goal.

The Third Step

Once you have set your objective, bend as many of your resources and as much of your energies to achieving it as fast as you can. The time may be very short now.

How Much Do You Want to Do? How Much Can You Do?

There are three levels of preparation presented in this guide:

☑ **3-to-7 Days** (3-5-7 Track)

This track means being able to take care of yourself for three days to a week during the inconvenience of the temporary loss of utilities or limited access to goods and services, usually due to a localized disaster. All the systems of civilized life are still intact and will be restored. You only need to muddle through until normalcy returns.

☑ **Foreign, Economic or Natural Disaster** (FEND Track)

This track means preparing for a badly depressed or unstable economy, regional natural disasters, social upheaval, terrorist attacks, or foreign wars, during which basic services become erratic, rationed, unavailable, or too expensive. The period of time might last for months or years, and the consequences are, at the least, life-altering in a disagreeable way and, at the worst, life-threatening.

☑ **Off The Grid** (OTG Track)

This track means preparing for a time when services and access to goods cease for an indeterminate period of time. You are on your own. Forget about changes to your life style—your very survival is in question.

Finally, this guide covers four other preparation needs:

☑ Having a **Go-Bag** ready in case you must leave your house at a moment's notice. The Go-Bag is designed to get you over the hump of the next few days or a week until you can organize the goods and services you need to restore stability to your life.

☑ Preparing for a **barter economy.** This is an extension of OTG that requires thinking ahead about resources that may help keep your family alive.

☑ Planning for your **pets.**

☑ Planning for a **garden.**

It Can Happen to You

Headline, New Zealand Herald, September 4, 2010
Mayor: Quake hit city "like an iceberg"

A 7.1 earthquake hit Christchurch, New Zealand's second largest city with about 450,000 people, at 4:35 a.m. on Saturday, September 4, 2010. Nearly every building in the city was damaged, some extensively. Roads were blocked by fallen debris and the center of the city looked like a "war zone." A state of emergency was declared and local officials were considering evacuating some parts of the city. Street surfaces were badly cracked and thrust up, and craters in the roads rapidly filled with water from ruptured mains. The airport was closed, rail service was shut down, and several major bridges were impassable.

City residents were asked to not flush the toilet, as the sewer system was damaged. Within hours panicked residents began lining up to buy water. Emergency services were flooded with calls, but they could respond only to serious cases because of widespread damage to roads and bridges. Hospitals were quickly inundated by injured persons. Residents with lesser injuries were asked to go to 24-hour clinics so the hospitals—themselves damaged—could focus on persons with more serious injuries.

One family, still in their pajamas, grabbed their dogs and hastily climbed into their car. The road was nearly impassable at times but they made it out safely.

The New Zealand earthquake was a classic 3-5-7 event with elements of FEND and OTG.

Some 450,000 New Zealanders went to bed in the "Old World" and woke up at 4:35 a.m. in a terrifying "New World." The terrible shaking lasted a few minutes and the aftershocks for a few days, but the ramifications of the "New World" would be around for weeks and months for many people.

☑ Some chose to flee at the height of the crisis, while others faced evacuation orders in the following hours or days. A Go-Bag stored in the car would have been invaluable in such a situation where they needed to move very quickly and couldn't return for a period of time.

☑ Streets blocked with debris, and damaged roads and bridges, prevented emergency medical personnel from reaching injured people. Hospitals were swamped, and people with non-life-threatening injuries were sent elsewhere. In a similar situation, people who had prepared could attend to their own non-life-threatening injuries so they could focus on what needed to be done next.

☑ Supermarkets and pharmacies were damaged, most of their contents smashed and unsalvageable. The power outages meant that frozen and refrigerated foods and meats were ruined. Food and drug deliveries in the near-term future would be restricted, and many important items would be unavailable or rationed until the power was returned, the buildings repaired, and roads cleared so deliveries could get through. Anyone who had stored some food would not need to worry for at least a week in a similar situation, and hopefully longer, if they had prepared for FEND and OTG. What was or was not on the supermarket shelves in the near future, and whether they could get it at any cost, was not a priority in the first days after the earthquake.

☑ The infrastructure of the city was heavily damaged, especially the sewer system and water distribution system. Clean drinking water became instantly unavailable and bathrooms unusable. In such a situation, people who had stocked water did not have to stand in any lines in the first few hours. In the Christchurch case, the water issue would extend into weeks (and perhaps months) as repairs of the infrastructure were going to take a while, making getting clean water to drink a critical issue into the future. Electricity was restored in about a week and, after that, those who had electric water distillers could make their own drinking water. Even those who remained without power for a longer time would still be able to purify drinking water and prepare food as long as necessary if they had prepared for the OTG track.

The Christchurch earthquake was a local catastrophe. Civilization and government services were still intact, just shaken up temporarily. Medical care was available, if delayed, and many support services and organizations swiftly stepped in to help the people of Christchurch cope and recover. Nevertheless, in one minute, the New Zealander's normal life crumbled, and normalcy would not return for some time to come.

Packing a Life Raft in Your Luggage for a Voyage on the Unsinkable *Titanic*

Most of us can stumble through three days to a week of inconvenience when we know it will pass, even if it is miserable at the time. But in a larger and more devastating catastrophe, how you have arranged to take care of yourself <u>in the first 72 hours</u> may make the difference between whether you get to anything <u>after the first 72 hours</u>.

In the first 72 hours after a crisis, what would you do if you could not:

- ☑ Access your bank account using your ATM card?
- ☑ Use your debit card or credit cards to purchase goods?
- ☑ Pay your bills on the computer or by check?
- ☑ Put gas in your car?
- ☑ Use your car at all, ever again?
- ☑ Make a phone call, including using your cell phone?
- ☑ Get food?
- ☑ Heat or cool your home?
- ☑ Get clean water from your tap?
- ☑ Remain in your home for the foreseeable future?
- ☑ Cook on your stove or in your microwave?
- ☑ Turn on the lights?
- ☑ Turn on your TV, radio, or computer to get news?
- ☑ Get medical care when someone in your family has a health emergency?
- ☑ Call the police in a crisis situation?
- ☑ Use your bathroom?
- ☑ Get vitally needed prescription drugs?
- ☑ Deal with medical emergencies on your own?
- ☑ Get a terrible toothache and there are no dental services available?

What would you do first? Rush to the grocery store to stock up on food and water? Wait in line at the bank to get a little cash before they ran out or the bank was closed for an unknown period of time? Wait in long lines at the gas station to get the last few gallons of gas so you can do any of the other errands or evacuate your family? Try to collect your family together? Desperately try to find medical help for injured members of your family? Scramble around trying to decide what to take with you if you have to leave your home?

Fortunately there are answers—admittedly not easy or happy ones—to the questions above. Unfortunately, they are disturbing to think about, hard to prepare for, and they will be even harder to live with if the worst happens.

Those who are prepared can use that <u>first 72 hours</u> to make reasoned life-saving decisions and set a new course for the future. They will not have to worry about what critical needs have to be dealt with first, or at all. You won't be the one scrambling for the last deck chair on the *Titanic*, critically behind the survival curve from the beginning, and hopelessly compromised for whatever comes <u>after 72 hours</u>.

But, seriously, what are my chances of needing to prep?

What is the percentage of possibility that you will have to deal with a three-day-to-one-week crisis without basic services and access to resources like food and clean water at some point in your life? 100%

☑ Those who wish to prep to this level should follow the <u>3-5-7 Track</u>. This track requires minimal input of time and budget. It is just common sense, as everyone will need it at one or more points in their lives.

What is the percentage of possibility that basic services and goods may become harder to get or even unobtainable, may be erratically provided or very expensive (if you can even get them) for months, perhaps even years? The world is on the edge. The possibility of a sharp, severe economic downturn (perhaps coupled with overwhelming natural disasters), or the possibility of foreign wars or external enemies striking us here is about 80%. What it will actually look like when it gets here is unknown. There are simply too many factors which are out of our hands to know for sure.

☑ The <u>Foreign, Economic or Natural Disaster (FEND) Track</u> is useful for those who think the dangers listed above are real. Food and other items can be used over the long term to defray rising costs and offset shortages or unavailability. This track requires a good deal of time and resources, and should not be undertaken lightly.

What about the ultimate catastrophe—a worst case scenario? A reasonable person counts it out altogether at his peril. The percentage may be as low as 5%, but if it happens, it is instantly 100%, possibly for a long period of time.

☑ The <u>Off The Grid (OTG) Track</u> is for people who want to be able to go it on their own. This track frees us from dependence on systems and services provided by others. It is the most complex, time-consuming, and expensive. But if your family is forced OTG, then every penny, drop of sweat, and moment of time invested will be a life-saver. Literally.

And, after all, what is the worst that could happen if the worst doesn't happen? What if the situation does improve and everyone ends up gamboling around like little bunnies in green fields full of flowers under a beautiful rainbow? Well, you've got a lot of extra stuff and you wasted some time and money. It's not the end of the world. But are you willing to bet your life, and the life of your family, on the gamboling bunnies scenario? I'm not.

Not convinced? You might want to take a little time and read two important books. Both are technically fiction.

☑ *One Second After* by William R. Forstchen. It is about what happens in the aftermath of an EMP (electromagnetic pulse) attack on the United States that in one second sends us all back to the Middle Ages. This book will change your life—and maybe save your life. The audio version is very powerful and I recommend it over the printed book. The audio book can be bought for $20 and the print version for about $15 from Amazon. Be warned though, this book is <u>grim</u>. Every time you think it can't get worse, it does, by about a factor of four, and there never seems to be a bottom. There is no happy ending here, no sitcom wrap up in 22 minutes or "it was all a dream" finish.

I guarantee that once you start, you will not be able to stop listening or reading. You will not think the same again.

☑ *World Made by Hand* by James Howard Kunstler. Call this book a sequel to *One Second After*, set about four or five years after a "one second after" event. It is a different setting and a slightly gentler approach, but that's only because enough time has passed to soften the original catastrophe. Here is the OTG life—and it's not pretty. You can get it at Amazon for about $10.

These two books are unintentional companions. *One Second After* should be read first and then a *World Made by Hand*. If you are wavering about the need to prepare, these two books will cure you of it.

Our Life Support Systems and Services

We all depend on the following life support systems and services:

1. Water
2. Food
3. Medical/Dental
4. Security
5. Economics/Finances
6. Communications
7. Utilities
8. Household/Personal Hygiene
9. Transportation

Water, food, medicine, and security are the most important systems—the "Big Four." The rest are irrelevant if you die of thirst, starvation, or disease, or someone takes your life simply because you have something they need or just want. That is not to say the others are not important (they are) but, if your budget and time is limited, your attention must be placed on the Big Four.

Why This Book Is Unique

There are many books on the market about preparing for disasters and many about preparing in one system such as buying and storing food. They are good resources. But *Ready for Anything: The Ultimate No B.S. Survival Manual for Ordinary People* is unique. I wrote it because there was nothing like it available. You get to benefit from my research and my errors as I fumbled my way through the process. *Ready for Anything: The Ultimate No B.S. Survival Manual for Ordinary People* will tell you:

- ☑ Exactly what to purchase
- ☑ Where to get it
- ☑ How much it will cost
- ☑ Why you need it
- ☑ Keeps you organized along the way
- ☑ Provides detailed information and tips on a lot of hard-learned skills gleaned through hard work and research.

By using this guide, you can get prepared for ANY situation in as short a time as possible.

How To Use This Guide

☑ First, select the <u>track</u> most appropriate to the level of preparation you want to achieve.

☑ Each <u>system</u> has its own chapter. Read the general information for each system and then the part of the chapter on the track you have chosen.

☑ **Worksheets**, **shopping lists,** and **inventory forms** are provided for each life-support system so you can organize to achieve your goal quickly and efficiently.

The chart below makes it easy for you to access just the information you want for the preparation level you have chosen. You don't need to waste a lot of time researching and reading. Just acquire what the section says and use any of the tips provided that fit your situation.

	3-5-7	FEND	OTG
WATER	Section 1.1	Section 1.2	Section 1.3
FOOD	Section 2.1	Section 2.2	Section 2.3
MEDICAL/DENTAL	Section 3.1	Section 3.2	Section 3.3
SECURITY	Section 4.1	Section 4.2	Section 4.3
ECONOMIC/FINANCES	Section 5.1	Section 5.2	Section 5.3
COMMUNICATIONS	Section 6.1	Section 6.2	Section 6.3
HEATING/COOLING/LIGHTING/COOKING	Section 7.1	Section 7.2	Section 7.3
HOUSEHOLD/PERSONAL HYGIENE	Section 8.1	Section 8.2	Section 8.3
TRANSPORTATION	Section 9.1	Section 9.2	Section 9.3

There are four additional chapters:

☑ Building a Go-Bag
☑ Barter Economy
☑ Pets
☑ Gardening

This guide WILL provide you with the information needed to quickly and efficiently acquire the resources you need to survive in the track you choose. It will NOT provide you with information on the practical aspects of survival—for instance, the application of medical care, growing a garden, learning to can, chopping wood, or any other practical skills. The section "Building Your Survival Library" is provided at the end of the book and includes useful books on these subjects to expand your resource base.

A Final Note

Every day it gets clearer that the time may be growing short, so speed may be of the essence. You should choose your track and then start IMMEDIATELY and move FAST. Remember that, if something terrible does happen, the dividing line between civilization and chaos is 72 hours. However, it will take you a lot longer than 72 hours to prepare to cross the survival bridge across that chasm. If you decide to prepare, don't do it out of fear. Fear will not carry you through to the end of this project. Do it out of hope in the future.

If you have decided to pack a life raft in your luggage for your voyage on the unsinkable *Titanic*, congratulations! If the catastrophe is survivable, preparing will give yourself and your family the best chance at life. Good luck, and may God bless you in your 1,000 mile journey.

So let's get started!

The Need for Secrecy in Your Preparations

Irene Adler: *Why are you so suspicious?*
Sherlock Holmes: *How shall I answer? Chronologically or alphabetically?*
Sherlock Holmes (Movie, 2009)

You should tell NO ONE what you are doing—not your parents, or brothers and sisters, not your co-workers, not your best friends, not your neighbors. I realize that the suggestion that you maintain such secrecy makes me sound like I'm a suspicious person. I am not a suspicious person—I've blown right through suspicious, and I am deep into the land of paranoia.

It would be severely unwise to underestimate what the Powers That Be (PTB) will do when events spiral out of their control and they feel their power is slipping through their fingers. You can safely assume one thing: whatever they do, it won't be in our best interests but in theirs. Even if they did do something to help, it would be too little, too inept, too late and probably do far more damage than good overall since it will probably involve seriously astronomical spending. Whatever they do is likely to be swift, brutal, unconstitutional, and possibly deadly—but the reality is that the PTB have all the power, including the ability to arrest, imprison, and even kill you if they want. That's hard to imagine, I know, but try. The front men may seem like a bunch of clowns and corrupt cowards, however, those who are really running our country behind the scenes are utterly ruthless. Their power grab is like a very high-stakes chess game. If they are placed in check, they will probably not accept the next move—a checkmate—and just sweep all the pieces off onto the floor and then break the board in half. If they can't have it, then no one will. They have been waiting for their big moment for one hundred years. Do you really think that they're going to get queasy at the thought of crushing or condemning to death a bunch of faceless subjects to keep their power?

That nice lady from next door who always stops to talk with you as she walks her dog is not exempt from your concerns. If the system collapses, within 72 hours to one week, that woman will probably be desperate, crazy with hunger, and wild with fear for her family. If she knows you have something she needs to save her family, that lovely woman may not hesitate to try to take it from you. What about the members of the 44% of American households who are on some kind of government assistance as of 2010? If the money stops flowing, what will they do in their panic? And that's just the civilized people.

There are also plenty of animals who will quickly realize that the "New World" is their idea of paradise.

These are the ones who were barely kept in control by the police and justice system, and to whom robbery, rape, and murder are sport, and who are now free to do as they wish. They'll do it to you and your family without even batting an eyelash.

You should keep in mind that the fastest and easiest way someone can get out from under trouble themselves is to direct their persecutors to someone else. And if that someone is you, you could lose everything you have worked so hard for and so carefully obtained, up to and including your life, in the space of a couple of hours. In Poland during the Holocaust, Poles turned in Jews—and their fellow Poles—to certain death for a single loaf of bread or a few coins.

So keep your preparations inside your immediate family. If you have children, tell the young ones that you are preparing for an "adventure" in case there is a big storm. Tell the older children, who can see that what you are doing is beyond preparing for a five-day power outage, to tell NO ONE. Impress upon them that their life and the lives of their family may depend on it. Make them understand that they can't chat about it idly with school friends or teachers, Twitter about it on their phone, or blog about it on the computer. <u>They must be silent</u>.

In the event of a disaster, you well may choose, with good will and compassion, to share your food and preparation tools with your family or others, but do it quietly. Never show anyone your full food stock or the extent of your preparations— before or after the event. If you do decide to confide in someone else, or to throw in your lot with them to improve your outlook—do so ONLY if you KNOW that you can trust them with your LIFE, because that is what it comes down to in a serious, long-term disaster.

Civilization is a very thin veneer. Civilization is not just the culture, art, and social arrangements of a group of people. It is an agreement by most of the members of a community to abide by certain rules so that all may thrive in security and stability. Those who do not abide by the rules are punished by the members of the community. When the rules disappear, so does civilization. Remember how we watched in horror as it broke down in just a few days right in front of our eyes on our TVs in the aftermath of Hurricane Katrina?

This does not mean you should eye everyone as though they were your mortal enemy all the time. But it is wise not to count out that, under the right circumstances, they could be. It would be reckless indeed to give them the power to hurt you before the real struggle even begins.

And remember—silence is golden—in this case literally!!

WATER

It is only when they go wrong that machines remind you how powerful they are.

~Clive James~

Chapter

1

What if...?

The first scenario isn't just possible—it has already happened to me.

A severe thunderstorm hit my part of town. After a singularly bad lightning strike and thunder clap—the kind that comes right together and sounds like the roof just fell in—I noticed that I had lost water pressure in the taps. The lights flickered, but came right back on. The water came back full force after some sputtering, about ten minutes later. Like a fool I was just grateful the problem was fixed and continued to use the water.

Twenty-four hours later I learned from the news that the local water treatment plant had been knocked off-line for a few minutes by a lightning strike, and the authorities were advising people to boil the water before using it. I learned about the boil advisory as I lay in bed, sick from some kind of a stomach thing, listening to the radio. Clearly there had been no comprehensive or timely plan in place for advising people about issues involving water quality. (The lesson learned was not to count on government to inform you about potential water quality problems, but to use your common sense and err on the side of caution. I wish I had.)

Too late I turned to bottled water, which I had on hand. However, it was very hard to remember not to use the tap. Every time I turned around, I was reaching for the faucet handle. I'd wash my hands, rinse out a cup, or pick up my toothbrush, and then realize I couldn't do that. Finally I wrapped socks over the faucets so that I would remember not to use them. It was the only way to catch myself in time from turning on the tap. [Try it. Put something around your faucets for a day, or even a few hours, and then watch how often you and your family try to use them. I guarantee it will surprise you.]

Drinking was no problem as I had bottled water, but what about washing the dishes? I switched to paper plates, plastic cups, and cutlery to keep the dishes from piling up in the dishwasher. What about washing my hands and face? Washing up in the kitchen? Preparing food? What about my pet's drinking needs?

It is also worth noting that, in a trip to the grocery store one day after I finally heard about the boil advisory, I found that bottled water was completely unavailable. The shelves were empty.

Finally, after four days, we were advised that it was safe to drink the water. However, I wasn't sure how many times I had to run the dishwasher before the water in the pipes was clean again. How long did I have to run the faucets before I could trust the water to be clean again?

What if the emergency lasts longer than a few days?

In 1993 the largest waterborne disease outbreak in United States history broke out in Milwaukee, Wisconsin. The municipal water supply had been contaminated by *Cryptosporidium* eggs that passed through the filtration system of one of the city's water-treatment plants.

This abnormal condition at the plant lasted from March 23 through April 8, after which, the plant was shut down. Over the span of approximately two weeks, 403,000 of an estimated 1.61 million residents in the Milwaukee area became ill with stomach cramps, fever, diarrhea, and dehydration caused by the pathogen. Over 54 deaths were attributed to this outbreak, mostly among the elderly and immunocompromised people, such as AIDS patients.

In a similar case, an electric distiller could save your life, or at least keep you from becoming very sick.

Finally, what if—in the wake of a major hurricane, flood or earthquake for instance—the ground water was contaminated, the treatment plants were off-line for the foreseeable future, or the infrastructure was damaged and you had no utilities for the foreseeable future? Your bottled water will run out soon, the electric distiller is a lump of inert metal. Now what?

GENERAL INFORMATION

The Number One Survival Need

Clean drinking water is the single most critical item to have or be able to obtain reliably in the event of any emergency. It is absolutely essential to survival. A human being can live for a relatively long time on reduced food rations, but only about three to four days without water.

Excluding fat, water composes approximately 70% to 75% of the human body by mass. It is critical to the metabolic process. Dehydration occurs when you lose more water than you take in. The elderly, infants and children, and sick people are more at risk for dehydration.

Even mild dehydration can slow down your metabolism as much as 2% and can trigger fatigue, dizziness, fuzzy short-term memory, trouble with basic math, and difficulty focusing. Mild dehydration can be stabilized by drinking fluids. Moderate to severe dehydration (10% and higher) requires immediate medical attention. Muscle cramps, nausea, vomiting, and heart palpitations can lead to coma and death.

What makes water contaminated?

Any surface or rain water in the United States should be considered unsafe to drink without treatment. Even if the water is clear and smells and tastes good, that does not mean it is safe to drink. Clear cold mountain streams can contain *Giardia* or *Cryptosporidium,* which make their way into surface water via animal feces. Agricultural areas are even more severely contaminated with these two organisms since cattle are a major carrier. Water in urban areas can also be contaminated by septic systems, sewers, industrial plant pollution, and so on.

There are many types of contaminants in water:

☑ Bacteria are single-celled organisms. One bacterium can multiply into millions in just a few hours. Cholera, salmonella and some varieties of *E. coli* are bacteria. They are so small that only filters rated <u>0.2 microns</u> <u>or less</u> can filter them out.

☑ Protozoa are single-celled animals. Unlike bacteria, they can move around on their own. However, protozoa are generally larger than bacteria (3 to 10 microns) so it is easier to filter them out.

They are tricky though, because in harsh conditions, they change into cysts (eggs in a hard cover). The protective cover of the cyst allows them to survive in a dormant state until they encounter growth conditions again—like inside you. Then they return to their active form and begin to multiply. It is the cyst form that is very difficult to kill with iodine or bleach. Only boiling or distilling will kill the cysts.

☑ Viruses are also different than bacteria and are even smaller, and so can get through most filters. Some waterborne viruses are hepatitis A, polio and Norwalk virus.

☑ Parasites can be microscopic in size and include malaria and trichinosis.

☑ Metals such as arsenic and lead from industrial pollution.

☑ Inorganic compounds are large molecules such as gasoline, solvents, pesticides, latex paint and plastics.

☑ Other contaminants can be pesticides, fluoride, mercury, nitrates, radium (radioactive), and radon.

Methods of Killing or Removing Contaminants

The following chart shows what treatments kill or remove the various types of contaminants:

CONTAMINANT	DISTILLING	BOILING	CHEMICAL	ULTRA VIOLET	PORTABLE FILTERS
Bacteria	Yes	Yes	Yes	Yes	Uncertain
Protozoa	Yes	Yes	Not certain	Yes	Uncertain
Viruses	Yes	Yes	Yes	Yes	Uncertain
Parasites	Yes	Yes	Not certain	Yes	Uncertain
Metals	Yes	No	No	No	Yes
Inorganic compounds	Not certain	No	No	No	Yes
Others	Not certain	No	No	No	Yes

What You Need to Know about *Cryptosporidium*

Cryptosporidium (and other related protozoa such as *Giardia*) are tricky to kill because in harsh conditions they grow a protective cover (a cyst) and settle down into a dormant state until they encounter growth conditions again. Then they return to their active form and begin to multiply.

Cryptosporidium cysts are very hardy and can survive a 24-hour soak in undiluted bleach!! *Cryptosporidium* is what made it through the chlorination process in Milwaukee, Wisconsin in 1993, sickening hundreds of thousands of people and killing 54. The main symptom is diarrhea, which in persons with a compromised immune system (the elderly, young, or sick) can be fatal. This is not something to mess with in a world that may have little or no medical care.

In both their active and cyst form, they resist most chemical treatments and can only be killed for certain by boiling or distilling the water. Only Aquamira and Micropur (both of which are a two-part chlorine dioxide water treatment) ARE guaranteed to kill all organisms, including cysts, in 5 to 10 minutes.

What is the Difference between Boiled Water and Distilled Water?

Distilled water is created by boiling water in a closed compartment in a distiller which produces water vapor. The water vapor condenses on a cool surface which then condenses back into a liquid. The condensed liquid is deposited in a clean container outside the distiller. The condensed steam vapor is what you drink. Distilled water is about 98% to 99.9% pure. Since distilling removes all minerals from water, some feel that drinking distilled water over a long period of time is not a good thing because the magnesium, calcium and other minerals in the tap water are beneficial for the body. Others disagree, believing you get all the minerals you need from your food.

Boiled water is water that is heated to the full boiling temperature of 212°F at sea level. Boiling points vary depending on the altitude. Some people claim that as little as 140°F is enough to kill most micro-organisms but, to be on the safe side, the water should be brought to a rolling boil for several minutes. Boiling is the only fool-proof way to inactivate or kill most micro-organisms. Boiled water must still be filtered to remove any inorganic, chemical or industrial contaminants. You then drink the boiled and filtered water itself.

How Much Water Do You Need?

It is a common misconception that everyone should drink about 64 ounces of water per day (about two quarts or eight glasses.) This idea is not supported by scientific research. In fact, no one even seems to know from where this "rule of thumb" came.

The amount of water each human being needs varies. Government studies recommend that <u>at minimum</u>:

- ☑ Males older than 18 should take in a minimum of about 125 ounces (8 pints or so).

- ☑ Females older than 18 should take in a minimum of about 90 ounces (5.5 to 6 pints).

- ☑ Sick people need more water. Fever, vomiting or diarrhea causes the body to lose fluid which needs to be replaced.

  (On the other hand, some conditions such as kidney, liver, and adrenal diseases may impair excretion of water and even require limiting fluid intake.)

- ☑ Women who are pregnant or breastfeeding need more fluids. Women who are pregnant should drink at least twelve 8-ounce cups of water per day, and those who are breast-feeding should consume about thirteen 8-ounce cups of water per day.

TIPS:
We also get water from food and beverages. However, your body needs water to digest food, so if your water intake is limited, try to also limit your intake of dried foods as much as possible.

Ultimately, how much water a person needs depends on the person's health, the amount of physical exercise they do, and the environmental temperature.

A simple Human Water Requirement Calculator can be found at: http://www.csgnetwork.com/humanh2owater.html. Enter your weight, amount of exercise and the type of climate. The results are approximate but they will give you a baseline for calculating your water needs.

Don't forget, we also use water for:

☑ Cooking
☑ Washing ourselves
☑ Washing dishes, clothing, and other household tasks

You should add 50% to your water calculation for each person to account for cooking, light washing up of your person, dental care, washing dishes, and hand laundering of small items of clothing.

Don't forget your pets when calculating water storage. A large dog or other animal could add substantially to your stockpile requirements.

Quick Facts: Measurements

☑ 1 average-sized bottle of water is about 1 pint (they vary)
☑ Thus about 8 average-sized bottles (1 pint) of water = 1 gallon
☑ 1 pint = 16 ounces
☑ 8 pints = 1 gallon = 128 ounces

Additional Water Sources in an Emergency

You also have some backup water sources in your house:

☑ In a pinch, you can drain your water heater, boil it, and drink it. (Turn off the gas or electric power first or you will damage the heater.)

☑ You can use the water from the toilet tank (NOT the bowl). Don't use the water in the tank if you use a toilet product from the store in it.

☑ If you have warning about the emergency, you may also wash out the bathtub with a mild solution of bleach and water, and fill it up. However, tap water that sits for awhile in an open source will still need to be boiled as it will get bacteria in it.

☑ You may also fill any container you have around, including wastebaskets. First line them with two plastic garbage bags.

☑ The pipes in your home can also be drained. Open the highest tap slightly and drain the water from a lower tap.

☑ If you have a swimming pool, it can provide a source of water for some time, but it has to be <u>treated</u> before drinking—no matter how much like chlorine it smells.

Buying Bottled Water

Cases of bottled water come in many different sizes and contain different numbers of bottles. Generally, most of the medium-sized bottles are about one pint each. Most stores also carry gallon bottles of water. The cases will be labeled with the number of bottles in it, amount in each bottle, and a total gallon figure.

☑ Every time you go to the grocery store, bring home at least 2 cases.

☑ Watch for sales offered by stores on various brands.

☑ Read the label which summarizes how much is in each by bottle, the number of bottles in the case, and the total gallon figure. Use the gallon figure. It's easier than trying to keep track of 778 pints of water across a stack of various-sized cases and brands. If the case insists on telling you everything in liters and milliliters, move on and buy another kind, if you have a choice. This is America: we don't do metric.

☑ Get some gallon jugs of water as well.

TIP:
Try to get some gallon bottles with real handles that you can put your fingers through, and air tight caps (not the flip up kind). Save them, because in the FEND and OTG tracks, you can use them to collect or store more water or other items. If and/or when plastic jugs become unavailable, they will be priceless. The jugs with handles are easier to carry, singly or in multiples, and you can tie them to something if you have to move water—which is heavy.

☑ Don't buy the square gallon jugs with the spigots on the side because they leak over time.

> ***Prepper's Rule #1: You can never have too many bottles and jars!*** After you have used the contents of smaller bottles or jars, save them too. In fact, save any container that seals tightly, especially if it is glass. These can serve many useful purposes over time.

☑ Use the **Water Inventory Sheet** (Appendix C) to keep track of how much water you are accumulating. Date it, number the case, and put the water someplace cool.

☑ Don't wait until the last minute to buy bottled water. It's heavy and bulky to haul home if you need a lot of cases, and it may not be available at all in a crisis.

Storing Water

You should store your water someplace cool if possible. Water in plastic bottles may acquire a plastic taste over time, but the water is still all right to drink.

Using the Forms

☑ Use Worksheet #1: **Family Water Calculator Worksheet** (Appendix A) to determine how much water, in gallons, your family needs.

☑ After you have purchased water, use the **Inventory Sheet: Water** (Appendix C) to list your purchases.

SECTION 1.1: WATER 3-5-7 TRACK

Goal: To provide your family with drinkable water for a short-term emergency.

There are three steps to providing you and your family with adequate clean drinking water in a short-term emergency.

Step 1:

Use the **FAMILY WATER CALCULATOR WORKSHEET** (Appendix A) to determine how many gallons of water your family needs each day. Multiply the total gallon number for your family by the number of days for which you wish to have emergency bottled water on hand. (The full seven days is recommended, if your budget permits.)

Step 2:

Buy it and store it someplace cool. While you are at the store, buy some paper plates, bowls, cutlery, and cups. That will keep down the need to wash dishes during the emergency.

Step 3:

Use the **WATER INVENTORY SHEET** (Appendix C) to keep track of your purchases. If you store them in different places or off-site, you won't have to keep counting them all the time, trying to remember what you have already. Also you may want to date the cases because, after a few months, the water will start to taste like plastic. You might as well use up the older ones first, or use one or two cases regularly and replace them.

That's it! You are done for 3-5-7.

SECTION 1.2: WATER FEND TRACK

Goal: To be able to purify enough water for your family for an indefinite period of time.

When the tap water is tainted and the bottled water is gone, you will need an electric distiller. Being able to use an electric distiller assumes that the water distribution system is damaged, but you have electricity, as occurred in the Christchurch, New Zealand earthquake. The power was restored in about one week, but the repairs to the water and sewer mains infrastructure took several months due to the severity of the damage underground.

TIP:
If you are concerned that you might have neither drinkable water nor utilities for the duration of a long-term emergency, and your budget is limited, you may want to go straight to the OTG non-electric distiller. You can always get an electric distiller later if time and budget allows, but in the meantime, you will have water for a long period whether you have utilities or not. It just won't be as easy to produce as with an electric distiller.

The wonderful thing about a water distiller is that it gets almost all of the contaminants out of the water in one process. The exceptions are inorganic compounds from industrial pollutants such as gasoline. They are volatile and evaporate along with the steam and then re-condense in the purified water. However, good distillers have one last defense against these holdouts—they incorporate a carbon filter between the steam chamber and the collection carafe to filter out the last of the impurities. However, not even distillation will kill prions (i.e., mad cow disease, scrapie, etc.). Fortunately, they are very rare.

What To Look For In An Electric Distiller

A quick search of the Internet reveals a bewildering number of electric *water* distillers in a variety of features and styles. The prices range from $200 to $300, but they can go higher. There are cheaper electric distillers available, but remember that you are dealing with very hot *water* and steam. It may be running nearly continuously for an undetermined amount of time, so it needs to be of high quality and durability.

Most of the electric water distillers that cost less than about $500 have a one-gallon capacity every 4 hours or so. One carafe will provide enough water for two individuals per day, if usage is carefully watched. That means, if you ran it for twenty-four hours straight, you could get six gallons of water. If you have a large family you may need to go to the more expensive models which can distill more water every day in less time.

When deciding which water distiller to buy, you should take into account the following factors:

- ☑ How much water do I need to distill on a daily basis?

- ☑ The collection container should be glass.

- ☑ The inside boiling chamber and distillation coil MUST be made of all stainless steel for durability. Remember you are dealing with a machine that may constantly be handling temperatures of at least 212°F. Only stainless steel will last through that brutal process.

- ☑ Carbon filters between the steam chamber and carafe are used to take out any final impurities in the water that may have escaped the steam chamber. Cheap distillers may use paper filters, which are useless. Good distillers use activated carbon (charcoal) to catch the last of the impurities.

 TIP:
The manufacturer's estimate of filter life is based on fairly gentle use—maybe a gallon a day—of tap water that is already relatively clean (at least as compared to a puddle of rain water or the smelly creek out back.) Filters will need to be replaced more often if the distiller is going to be used heavily on a daily basis. Reduce the estimated filter life accordingly, and stock up on extra filters. Also get some proper cleaner to clean out the steam chamber as there will be a buildup of left-behind contaminants on the inside surface and coil. Clean the distiller regularly and thoroughly, especially if it is heavily used. You should also order an extra glass carafe if possible.

Final Recommendations for the FEND *Water* Track

☑ My recommendation is a distiller from H2O Labs. You can check out their products at www.h2olabs.com.

☑ You might want to get several big bottles of vitamins too. If your after-catastrophe diet is different or rationed, you may have trouble getting enough basic minerals from your food or distilled water.

 TIP:
Only use the clean collection carafe for the final pure water. Use other containers when handling the contaminated water. Do not wash the collection container in contaminated water.

☑ You should still purchase some bottled water. If a crisis happens, there will be many difficult and stressful situations to deal with in the first days. Bottled water will get you over the hump and give you a little time to start a long-term water plan.

That's it! You're done for the FEND track!

SECTION 1.3: WATER OTG TRACK

Goal: To be able to produce drinkable water without utilities for an indeterminate amount of time.

TIP:
Go directly to Amazon and buy a copy of *When Technology Fails: A Manual for Self-Reliance, Sustainability, and Surviving the Long Emergency*, Revised and Expanded by Matthew Stein ($30.00). It is by far and away the finest book on this subject out there. Spend the money to get it overnight, if you can afford it. Go now. I'll wait. You can thank me later.

Back? Excellent. Let's begin.

Option 1: The Best Solution: A Non-Electric Water Distiller Coupled With an Efficient Alternative Heat Source

This is a one-step solution that requires two items:

1. A non-electric water distiller, and
2. An alternative heat source

The heat source is easy. You should purchase the Crisis Cooker from Solutions from Science. You can read about it and order it at www.crisiscooker.com. This unique stove can use charcoal, wood, or propane and can be instantly set up. Its patented heat chamber conducts heat ten times more efficiently than conventional stoves. Obviously it must only be used outdoors. It is portable, weighs 26 pounds, and is made of 18-gauge steel. The price is reasonable—about $180 including shipping. The really good news is that the Crisis Cooker also satisfies your OTG cooking needs, so it is a real bargain in the end.

However, any heat source will work, including campfires, grills, or portables stoves. Portable stoves and grills are readily available from sports, camping, or hiking equipment suppliers, as well as most department stores. However, be sure you don't buy any stove or grill that is fueled only by propane, kerosene, or white gas. You need something that can use wood or charcoal—hence the beauty of the Crisis Cooker. With the others, when the fuel is gone, so is your ability to cook food and boil water.

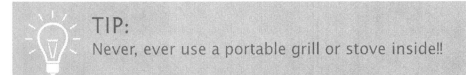

TIP:
Never, ever use a portable grill or stove inside!!

Finding a Non-Electric Distiller

Non-electric water distillers are very hard to find. The best one (and the one I own) is the Waterwise Model 1600. It is the perfect companion to the Crisis Cooker. They fit together like they were custom designed to do so. Together they ensure that, so long as there is physical water around, you will be able to treat it and drink it. Sadly, this item is no longer available. If you do find the *Water*wise Model 1600 (or for that matter, ANY non-electric distiller) anywhere—gathering dust on a store shelf, for sale on the Internet, in a rummage sale—do not slow down, GET IT! Then tie a big, mean, hungry dog with lots of teeth and a bad attitude to it to guard it, because it is worth its weight in gold.

After the Waterwise Model 1600 you have three options for purchasing a non-electric water distiller:

☑ Wholesale Water Distillers in Ohio. Their web site is: www.wholesalewaterdistillers.com. Select the "emergency water distiller." You can also order it by calling 740-544-5842 and conducting your business the old-fashioned way—talking to actual people. The current price is $320. They claim they will be able to supply them indefinitely and in any amount, but you should expect a "first come first serve" policy for this item.

☑ Water Distillers USA. As of this writing, they had only about 20 to 25 available and no intention of carrying it any more. You might get lucky, or they might change their mind about the profitability of this product. You can find it at www.waterdistillersusa.com.

☑ Finally, there is a unique item called the Life Saver Water Distiller from Conquest International. Their website is www.conquestinc.com/products/nonelectricdistiller.html. You can buy the kit and coil separately ($191 and $126 respectively) or the kit, coil and steam pot for $408.

I cannot recommend any of these three items personally as I do not own them. After you read the rest of this chapter which details the processes you have to go through to purify water without a non-electric water distiller, I think you will want one. If so, check out all three before making a decision so you get the one that is best for you. Remember, it will be "first come first serve" as the demand may outstrip the available stock very quickly.

You can build your own distiller. Moonshiners have done it for years—they just distill alcohol instead of water. Some favor solar distillers. It isn't difficult to make your own solar distiller, but the yield will be small and, of course, you need steady sunshine. You should also know that many argue that solar distillers aren't as effective as their proponents claim, as the temperature may not get high enough to destroy all biological contaminants.

TIP:
Unlike most electric distillers, non-electric distillers usually do not have one last carbon filtering system between the unit and the carafe. You must filter the water one last time through a carbon-filter system (discussed below) to remove the last traces of chemicals and inorganic compounds.

Instructions for making solar distillers or stills can be found on the web in profusion. You might want to look up the instructions before you lose access to the Internet.

Option 2: What To Do When You Can't Buy a Non-Electric Water Distiller At Any Price

Remember, if you cannot get a non-electric distiller, then water must be treated in a two-step process:

1. The water must be boiled and/or chemically or UV treated to kill biological contaminants.

2. It must then be filtered again to remove mineral, chemical or other toxic compounds.

Step 1: Removing Biological Contaminants

There are several ways to kill or inactivate contaminants:

- ☑ Boiling
- ☑ Manual chemical sterilization with chlorine or iodine
- ☑ UV (ultraviolet) sterilization
- ☑ Portable water filters.

Boiling

The only effective way to kill or inactivate most biological organisms is boiling. Some believe that heating water to between 140º F to 160º F (the temperature at which milk is pasteurized) is perfectly effective. However, to be safe, the water should be heated to a vigorous rolling boil (212º F) for several minutes, although technically, by the time the water reaches a rolling boil, the organisms should be dead. (However, just looking at the creek behind my house with its oily, smelly brown water with soapsuds curling on its surface makes me nauseous. If I had to use that water without benefit of a distiller, I would boil it until it was limp and then still put it through a strong filtering process afterward.)

Remember that boiling does not remove inorganic compounds or toxic chemicals. Nor does boiling remove bad smells or tastes.

You will need the following supplies to boil water:

- ☑ The Crisis Cooker or similar heat source and a large sturdy metal pot with a cover.

- ☑ A finely-woven cloth to initially filter bugs, twigs, sand, etc. out of the untreated water.

- ☑ Two sets of containers for collecting the contaminated water and storing the purified water. Keep them separate and don't wash the final collection containers in contaminated water.

>
> TIP:
> There is another excellent book called *Dare to Prepare!* (3rd edition) by Holly Drennan Deyo, which also deals in depth with water purification techniques and products. You can get it at www.daretoprepare.com. Click on the picture of the boo~~~~~~~~~~~~~~~~~~ the Table of Contents and ordering informa~~~~~~~~~~~~~~~~~~ipping. This book is over 600 pages long an~~~~~~~~~~~~~~~~~~e book for all OTG survival skills.

mms

Chemical sterilization

Contaminated water can also be treated .... to kill biological contaminants, both of which, some say, leaves a chemical taste. Some argue that the chemicals themselves may be damaging over the long term.

Chemical treatments, usually iodine in crystallized form combined with activated charcoal filters, are used by backpackers or travelers because they are inexpensive and light. The assumption is that the hiker is taking water from a mountain stream or a similar source that it is not extremely contaminated from the start. This may not necessarily be true for rainwater run-off from your roof or the local stream in an urban setting. Travelers also use chemical water treatments to purify water in countries where there is a questionable water purity issue.

Both bleach and iodine are easy to apply, readily available, and reasonably inexpensive for short-term use. Both chlorine and iodine can be purchased in pre-measured tablets or liquid form, or you can purchase the raw materials yourself. Chlorine is just regular bleach with no scents or additives (although it should be a 5.25% solution) and the iodine must be a 2% solution. The good part about buying pre-packaged chlorine or iodine is that you know exactly how much to put in the water, whereas measuring the correct amount from a bottle is harder. Further, the success of these methods is dependent on their being applied in the proper amount, under the correct conditions, and for the proper length of time. It is important to know, however, that most chemical treatments (except Aquamira and Micropur) are not 100% effective against *Cryptosporidium* in the cyst forms.

The wisest choice is to boil the water, then treat it with Aquamira or Micropur to remove any last biological holdouts.

Chemical Sterilization Products

Iodine-Based Products

    ☑ Polar Pure comes in tablet and liquid form and is pure crystallized iodine. The manufacturer claims that one bottle can purify nearly 2,000 quarts (500 gallons) of *water*. Polar Pure claims that it has been EPA tested in laboratory conditions and can kill cysts.

TIP:

Manufacturers' claims should be taken with a grain of salt. Every manufacturer tests their products differently, and believing that the EPA's guidelines are sacrosanct could be hazardous to your health. You may recall that the fabled FDA, the "watchdog of food purity," was so busy worrying about putting calorie counts on vending machines that they completely missed the salmonella problem in eggs, and 500,000,000 eggs had to be recalled. I don't know about you, but this does not inspire great confidence in me about claims of being "up to government standards."

Chlorine Dioxide Products

    ☑ Aquamira, available in tablet or liquid form, and Micropur in tablet form, are the only chemical products which can kill cysts. Both are based on a chemical compound called "chlorine dioxide" and the water tastes better than that treated with chlorine or iodine. However, they can only treat relatively small amounts of water per tablet or drop, and so could get quite expensive to stock for a long-term emergency. There are perfect for your Go-Bag though.

Chlorine

Chlorine is just household bleach without any additives or scents but it can also be purchased in tablet form. Read the label carefully, as some products sold as "bleach" are not chlorine at all. You can find the details about using bleach and iodine in Matthew Stein's book, *When Technology Fails,* and Holly Drennan Deyo's *Dare to Prepare!*

You may check out their products and claims at:

- ☑ Polar Pure: www.polarequipment.com
- ☑ Micropur: www.katadyn.com
- ☑ Aquamira: www.aquamira.com
- ☑ Chlorine tablets: www.katerno.com (and others).

TIP:
You don't want to use the chlorine tablets that are used to purify pool water for purifying drinking water. They might be handy if you have a pool you wish to use as a future drinking water source and you want to keep it as clean(er) for as long as possible. Water from a swimming pool must still be treated before drinking, no matter how much it smells like chlorine.

None of these products, including Aquamira and Micropur, remove the chemical, organic, or industrial pollutants in the water.

UV Sterilization

This product is called the "SteriPEN" and is available from Amazon. It has a UV (ultraviolet) lamp with a timer. It can treat small amounts of water in seconds and kills all bacteria, viruses and protozoa.

The problem is that the water must be clear so the light can shine through it, otherwise the sterilization will not be complete. It is excellent for travelers who want to treat their drinking water in countries with questionable water purity issues. It also uses batteries, so you will need a battery recharger and a supply of batteries for long-term disinfection. (Batteries and chargers will be dealt with in the "Communications" chapter.) A SteriPEN costs between $50 and $150.

Step 2: Filtering the remainder of the contaminants out.

So one way or the other, you have killed all the nasty little bugs and beasties that might kill you in your jug of rainwater, but what do you do about the last chemical and inorganic contaminants that might also kill you, but maybe just a little slower?

There is a bewildering number of water filtration devices on the market. They can be considered by type and function:

- ☑ Water filtration systems sold in department stores such as Brita, Pur, etc.
- ☑ Portable filters for campers and hikers
- ☑ Non-portable, heavy usage, gravity-fed units
- ☑ Low-tech natural filters

It is important to understand that these water filtration systems <u>do next to nothing</u> to filter out very small biological organisms such as viruses and bacteria which can make it through the filters. These filter systems are designed to catch non-biological contaminants (metals, toxic chemical, inorganic, etc.)

Let us consider each in turn.

Portable Water Filtration Systems (such as Brita and Pur)

Some of these filtration systems attach to your faucet or inside your refrigerator, and some are pitcher systems through which you pour the water independent of your tap. It is important to understand that:

- ☑ These filters are designed to further purify already drinkable tap water of its final non-biological contaminants. You cannot pour a bucket of rain water through it—even several times—and expect to get safe drinking water, because they do virtually <u>nothing at all</u> about microscopically-sized biological contaminants.

- ☑ They need replacement filters periodically. The filter's life is predicated on gentle use and relatively unpolluted water. Badly contaminated water may require several passes and, with each pass, the filter's life will be drastically shortened. Those who wish to use this method as the final filtration method will need to stock many replacement filters, and the number you need should be calculated on a much shorter filter life.

Zero Water is a pitcher system that contains a replaceable filter that is filled with activated charcoal and other technological filtering materials. It claims to remove the last contaminants in your water, right down to zero. I own this product and it does. But it requires a new filter every <u>22 gallons</u> and the manual clearly states that the results are based on <u>already potable</u> water that you just wish to make entirely pure.

In a long-term emergency, when, even after boiling, the water might still be contaminated with industrial and chemical pollutants, a filter won't last long at all and becomes less dependable as the filter nears the end of its life. The filters are not cheap either. (You can get four Zero Water filters from Amazon for about $50, and that is cheap compared to the price in the store.) Ultimately, a pitcher system is not a real long-term solution unless you can afford to stock a room full of filters.

So the final judgment on these filters is:

☑ For short-term emergencies using mildly contaminated tap water, they are excellent—assuming the water has already been biologically purified.

☑ For long-term emergencies, with heavy use and dirty water, they are a poor choice unless you can afford to stock a <u>large</u> supply of replacement filters.

TIP:
No matter what filter system you end up using, you need to invest in an electronic water tester. You dip it in the water, and it gives you a number reflecting the amount of Total Dissolved Solids (TDS). That is all it measures. The water could be teeming with bacteria, viruses and protozoa which are NOT measured and you won't be able to see. Nevertheless, a tester is a handy item to have for water that has been biologically purified and you wish to determine the level of chemical and inorganic pollution remaining. Zero Water gives you one with their pitcher, but you can order one from Amazon.

Other filters are designed for campers or hikers and therefore, are generally for short-term and small-volume use. The best ones use a cleanable ceramic cartridge with a carbon core. Ceramic filters can filter out some of the larger biological organisms, but not all, so some type of chemical or UV sterilization should be used on the filtered product to remove the last biological contaminants.

Portable filters range between $100 to $200 and the ceramic filters will need to be replaced at some point, although they last much longer than carbon filters. Matthew Stein and Holly Drennan Deyo discuss this subject at depth in their books, evaluating their various pros and cons and making recommendations. The two major manufacturers are MSR and Katadyn. MSR's filters are used by the military for purifying water in the field.

So the final judgment on portable filters is:

☑ A portable filter, together with a UV SteriPEN, is an excellent combination for your Go-Bag or to stash in your car in case you need to evacuate your home or are traveling.

☑ They are a better answer than pitcher filtration systems, but they are still not the answer for inexpensive long-term, high-volume decontamination of water.

Non-Portable, Heavy Usage Gravity-fed Units

These are a high-powered variant of the above filtration systems. Some are gravity-fed; that is, you pour the source water in the top and it emerges as purified water in a bottom reservoir. Others siphon the water from one container to another. Gravity-fed units require more time to produce clean water. Small biological organisms can still make it through these systems, so a SteriPEN or other chemical treatment should be applied to the filtered water for safety.

These units can produce many gallons per day over a long period of time. The ceramic cartridges still need to be replaced, but they last much longer. (They can process many thousands of gallons before the filter needs replacing.) They are not cheap, ranging in price from $300 to $1,200.

Matthew Stein deals in detail with the manufacturers, models, and various pros and cons of each in his book. He recommends Berkey, Katadyn, and AquaRain filters, but you should refer to his book for the details. Holly Drennan Deyo also explores this issue in detail in *Dare to Prepare!*.

So, the final judgment on non-portable, heavy usage, gravity-fed units is:

☑ They are the answer to long-term, high-usage water needs (although boiling the water should still be done for safety purposes) because their capacity and filter endurance is very high.

Low-Tech Natural Filters

Activated charcoal. This is used in many water filtration products to remove a wide variety of toxic compounds, and bad smells and tastes. Activated charcoal is NOT the briquettes in your grill. It is made from burned carbonaceous materials and then ground into a fine powder or pressed into a porous block.

It works by a process called *adsorption* (yes, that's spelled right)—that is, the surface area has millions of tiny nooks, crannies, and convolutions in which the contaminants get trapped. A teaspoon of activated charcoal has an adsorption surface area about equal to the size of a football field! It does great on pesticides and inorganic compounds, and removes bad tastes or smells. Activated charcoal has to be replaced when all the little nooks and crannies get filled up. You are not going to be able to tell this by looking at it, which is where a water tester will come in handy. When it starts registering significant Total Dissolved Solids (TDS), then it's time to change it out.

Activated charcoal in powdered form can be bought on the Internet at www.abnat. com. It ranges from $47 for 5 pounds to $264 for 44 pounds. Forty-four pounds would last practically forever. Matthew Stein's book, *When Technology Fails*, discusses how to construct such a filter.

Sand filters

If you live near a lot of sand, you can filter your water through several feet of sand laced with layers of activated charcoal. Sand, however, might not filter out some toxic pollutants and industrial chemicals.

Matthew Stein's book also discusses ways to find water and pump it out if necessary. (I told you it would be useful, didn't I? You're welcome.)

 TIP:
In an OTG situation, you should take steps to collect rain water. You can direct it into buckets from your downspouts or your roof, or collect rain in any variety of buckets or containers as rainfall. You can store what you collect in a larger barrel or collecting bin, like a plastic rolling garbage bin with a lid. And remember that all rain water must be treated.

Prepper's Rule #2: There is no such thing as having too many buckets or containers!! Get buckets or containers whenever you see them on sale— big ones, little ones, ones with air tight caps, flat ones, tubby ones, and ones with lids. In an emergency, yank the litter box out from under the cat, if necessary (wash it in bleach first, please). They will be useful in a thousand ways in the "New World." Put them all out when it rains.

A Final Note

You might be wondering why I went into all this detail. If you have significant disposable income, you can go directly to the web and purchase electric distillers, non-electric distillers, gravity-fed filters, SteriPENS, chemicals, replacement filters, and testers. An afternoon of work, a week or two for delivery, and you will have a complete water purification system for any emergency, no matter how long or severe.

However, most of us (including myself) are not in such an enviable financial position. We have to prioritize and economize. You may have to mix and match less expensive products, and add more layers and improvements to your system as it becomes possible. The above information should steer you away from poor, ineffective purchases and help you find the least expensive way to produce some kind of drinkable water, although it may not be perfect.

The above discussion should also have given you a healthy appreciation of the miracle our water purification systems are in the United States. We are the envy of nations around the world in which large percentages of their citizens suffer from waterborne diseases. You should think about that every time you flip on that tap, fill up a glass with clean water, throw in some ice, and drink deeply. You should regularly send a little prayer of thanks to the people who have developed and who maintain that precious resource for us. It should also be clear that if that system ever fails, especially for a significant amount of time, we will all be in for a great deal of sickness and work.

Final Recommendations for the OTG Track

Step 1:

Unless you intend to install, or have a wood stove in your home, buy a Crisis Cooker or some other portable stove (something that burns charcoal or wood).

Step 2:

If you decide you want to purchase a non-electric distiller, check the distributors and order the one you want.

Step 3:

If you decide to forego the non-electric distiller and boil your water, you should buy a big sturdy pot that fits on your chosen stove.

Buy two sets of basic supplies, such as funnels, thermometers, and jugs with air tight caps. You need two sets because you have to keep one for handling the clean water and one for the dirty water. Label them and do not mix them up.

Step 4:

If you feel you may not be able to boil water outside all the time, buy some Aquamira or Micropur as a backup. A SteriPEN is also a good buy for cleaning biological contaminants from clear (but not necessarily clean) water. Polar Pure also sells an inexpensive item called a Water Sock that you can use to filter the large debris out of water you take from sources such as streams, creeks, and rivers. The sock is used just to remove large sediment (sticks, leaves, dirt, sediments, bugs, etc.) to spare the strain on your chosen water filtration system. You can also use a closely-woven cloth for the same purpose. Otherwise the sock does NOT remove any other impurities. While you are at it, purchase a TDS electronic tester.

Step 5:

Finally, if you are really concerned about the purity of the final water, then purchase a non-portable, gravity-fed filter with adequate filters in reserve.

Step 6:

Purchase some activated charcoal. One bag will last for a long time, but get as much as you can afford.

Step 7:

Buy or recycle buckets and containers of every type to collect rainwater.

Step 8:

Don't forget to buy Matthew Stein's *When Technology Fails* and Holly Drennan Deyo's *Dare to Prepare!* so you know how to use it all.

That's it. You're done for the OTG level. I still recommend that you purchase some bottled water. If a crisis happens, there will be many critical things to deal with in the first days. Bottled water will get you over the hump and give you a little time to start a longer term water plan.

FOOD

There are only seven meals between civilization and anarchy.

~Spanish Saying~

Chapter

2

+ <u>China, December 18, 2009</u>

The Chinese authorities announced that food prices were going to increase. A panic was sparked and supermarkets in Beijing began to ration food items. Several elderly shoppers were injured in the rush to buy food.

+ <u>Great Britain, January 10, 2010</u>

Severe snow storms and freezing weather were predicted to sweep across Great Britain, and supermarkets were quickly stripped of essentials in anticipation of the storms. Within hours, the supermarket aisles were empty of bread, toilet paper, and frozen goods.

+ <u>Thailand, May 19, 2010</u>

Civil unrest tore Thailand apart for over three months and in May, curfews were imposed to control the violence in the street. One resident decided it might be wise to stock up on food and gas. Outside the supermarket, he found there was a "massive traffic jam." He drove on to another store where people were wildly buying up anything they could. He was only there five minutes before the store announced it would be closing, even though it was a 24-hour supermarket.

+ <u>Washington, D.C., February 6, 2010</u>

Before a massive blizzard hit, people mobbed the stores. The produce manager at one store said he had been in the grocery business for 24 years and had never seen such a "frenzy." People grabbed the produce from the shelves faster than he could put it on. Fortunately, a truck with fresh produce arrived before the entire department was empty. At other stores, the staff guarded the doors, only letting in more shoppers as other shoppers left.

The above are frightening occurrences, but they, and most others like them to date, relate to situations where the public panicked before a looming disruption: snowstorms, rumors of price increases due to shortages, floods, hurricanes, and the like. Anyone prepared for the 3-5-7 track would not have had to become part of those pushing, worried crowds grabbing anything they could get from the supermarket shelves before they closed.

More serious is a situation such as occurred in Thailand, where hundreds of thousands of demonstrators demanding a new election battled the government and the military, and turned Bangkok's streets into a battle zone between March and May 2010. The violence—some called it a civil war—quickly spread throughout Thailand, laid waste to its economy, and tore the country apart. The government censored radio, TV stations, and websites sympathetic to the demonstrators, and arrested their leaders, sparking new rounds of confrontation. The demonstrators set fire to banks, shopping centers, TV stations, and hotels, and detonated bombs all over the city. The confrontations died down after three months when the leaders of the demonstrators backed off, but several hundred demonstrators and soldiers had been killed, including two foreign journalists. The matter has still not been settled, and sporadic demonstrations continue. In the process, an estimated 100,000 people lost their jobs or their businesses, and experienced food and water shortages.

It is reasonable to assume that similar scenes are currently happening in England, Greece, and Ireland, and may spread to Portugal, Spain, and Italy as austerity budgets and increased taxes begin to take hold. If such a level of civil unrest occurred in major cities in the United States, many urban dwellers would quickly be in the same position as the Thais. Assuming one could stay out of the way of the two clashing sides, those who prepared for the FEND track would at least be able to ride out the shortages of food and water.

However, the most serious threats to the food supply of urban dwellers are not imminent natural disasters, or even the threat of social upheaval (as serious as that is), but arise from the structural fragilities in our food production and distribution systems. If the production or distribution system was seriously disrupted over a longer period of time than a few days, it could quickly lead to a serious long-term breakdown:

- ✦ The food on our supermarket shelves usually comes from thousands of miles away, whether in the United States or from foreign countries. Local warehousing is largely non-existent. Food is stocked "just in time", meaning the shelves are replenished as they are emptied. In a matter of hours or a day, a panicked population could empty the stores entirely and there would be insufficient replacements.

- ✦ Food production is heavily dependent on the use of fossil fuels to power the farm machinery necessary to plant and harvest crops, make fertilizers and pesticides, and to irrigate crops. All of these things have greatly increased the yield of a single acre of crops, making it possible to feed a growing global population. A disruption in oil supplies would impact adversely not only the food producers and crop yields but—more critically—could also sever the stretched-out link of transportation that connects the food producers and the consumers.

- ✦ Crop shortages caused by regional droughts or floods are nothing new; they have been around for thousands of years. Invariably, prices rise on the scarce commodity—sometimes steeply—but most crop shortages are healed in time by Mother Nature, the market and farmers' adaptability. This is not to say that shortages don't impact economies and lives—witness the food riots in Mozambique, Haiti, India, Egypt, China, and Mexico in recent years.

The larger problem is that the overall food production system is vulnerable because it is dominated by only a few crops. Maize (corn), wheat, rice, cotton, and soy comprise 91% of all the crops grown in the world. Wheat and corn are the two crops which impact the human food supply the most, either directly as, or in, the food we eat, as the base for animals feeds, or as seeds for next year's crop. This lack of diversity means that a serious disease in one crop like wheat could substantially impact food levels worldwide. One example of such a disease is called "stem rust" (Ug99) which is currently affecting wheat crops in Iran and Africa. Its cousin, "yellow rust," is taking a toll in North America, Australia, China, and Europe. In 2003 "yellow rust" wiped out a quarter of California's wheat crop. These crop pathogens can spread quickly and widely, and are genetically resistant to being controlled. If wheat rusts (or other crops diseases) start to affect crops worldwide, the shortages and resultant price increases will be far more severe—even in large industrialized nations such as the United States.

+ Government meddling and misguided ideological agendas can make a bad situation infinitely worse. Currently in the United Kingdom, over 80% of the costs of fuel are government taxes. In 2000, in a misguided attempt to restrict fuel consumption to combat dreaded "climate change," the government increased gas taxes significantly. There was a climate change all right—the public mood got ugly. Truck drivers blockaded oil refineries, demanding a reduction in the fuel taxes, which were threatening to drive them out of business. The protests spread and three-quarters of the gas stations had to be closed. Rumors flew that there would be no oil left in two days. The government refused to back down. Rolling roadblocks—trucks going deliberately slow—snarled traffic. Supplies were held for emergency use only. Supermarkets began to ration food and claimed it would all be gone in three days. The Royal Mail couldn't deliver the mail and schools closed. The government deployed the military to make sure oil and gas got to government-designated gas stations, and police escorted tanker trucks to their destinations. Although the protests petered out a few weeks later, in November 2000, the government eased the fuel taxes for the transportation industry.

+ It's not very helpful either that 25% of our corn crop is currently being turned to the manufacturing of ethanol, removing that amount of corn from the human food supply. If a squeeze in corn supplies comes, which is more important? More fuel to bring less food to market, or more food that never makes it to market because there is not enough fuel? Want to guess which side the green movement/government bureaucrats will come down on?

In Great Britain, the truckers stopped their protest voluntarily. But imagine a "Perfect Storm" no one could stop. A non-nuclear conflagration envelops the Middle East in which Iran closes the Straits of Hormuz to all tankers (and shiploads of grain and commodities too), crippling oil supplies around the world, including in the United States. Russia, China, India, Europe, and the United States vie brutally with each other to corner the market on non-Middle Eastern oil at any cost. Oil prices skyrocket, and fuel prices rise so sharply that it affects both the producers' ability to grow and harvest their crops and the distribution network that gets the results to our supermarket. Then just to make the situation worse, a major hurricane strikes the Texas coast, seriously disabling several important oil refineries. They will not be online again for several months. Impelled by the hurricane into an immediate crisis, the supermarkets are emptied of food, but this time there are no trucks arriving to bail them out. Government steps in to "smooth out" the problems—and as a consequence, the problems multiply exponentially. The economy—already teetering on the brink—implodes. Food riots erupt and people starve in the major cities, in the bread basket of the world.

NOTE: This scenario was written in October 2010. Doesn't sound so crazy now, does it? The Middle East is burning down or blowing up, in the midst of civil wars, and regimes have toppled or are toppling virtually overnight. Where the chaos ends is anyone's guess. The cost of a barrel of oil has spiraled up over $100. If Saudi Arabia falls into chaos, all bets about future food and transportation costs are off. There is most certainly a FEND situation in our future, perhaps even an OTG situation.

Are you ready?

GENERAL INFORMATION

There are two basic strategies for stocking large amounts of food for your family:

- ☑ You can buy the core of your food supply in freeze-dried form from the Internet. Then you can round off your core stock with items from the supermarket, or supplement it with bulk items such as grain.

- ☑ You can buy the core of your food supply in small amounts over time from the supermarket. Then you can supplement the supermarket food with freeze-dried items or with bulk items such as grain.

The way you decide to stock food will depend on your budget, time and food preferences.

The Pros and Cons of Both Strategies

Option 1: Buying Your Core Food Supply From a Pre-Packaged Food Dealer

Pro:

- ☑ It is a fast and efficient way to satisfy the bulk of your food requirements in one transaction.

- ☑ The food is freeze-dried and vacuum-packed so that it will last a long time (perhaps up to 25 years!).

- ☑ You can stock eggs, cheese, butter, fruits, and meats for long-term storage.

Cons:

- ☑ For a family of four, it can cost thousands of dollars up front for the food and shipping to stock up for any length of time (although a lot of these businesses are competing by offering free shipping).

- ☑ You need a lot of cool, dry storage space for large containers and boxes. A year's supply of food for a four-person family will fill a small room or large closet.

☑ If the Food Police come knocking on your door with an order from the Powers That Be to seize your "hoard" of food so it can be distributed "more fairly" by the government, pails, boxes, and large cans are a lot harder to hide in and around the average suburban home.

 TIP:
Some say the taste of freeze-dried food is atrocious. In my experience, this is not true. I have eaten Mountain View entrées; you add two cups of hot water, wait ten minutes, and you have a filling and delicious dinner. I can get two meals out of each entrée with no problem. Fresh food purists who swear by crispy fresh salads, crunchy vegetables, sprouts, seeds, and organic everything will understandably disagree— and they'd be right because the pre-packaged food is rich and a bit heavy. But in a FEND or OTG crisis, even a food purist will be able to force down freeze-dried food if nothing else is available. If they can't, they can always eat dandelion greens from the front lawn. But don't mind me if I watch from the porch as you're hunting for your dandelion greens, all the while I'm munching on my beef stroganoff and following it up with ice cream for dessert. Okay?

If you are concerned about the taste, then you should purchase a few entrées from a hiking and camping outfitter, or the camping section of the local department store (Walmart has Mountain View on sale in their camping section), and test it yourself. Or you can order a few samples from the Internet and taste them. There is no doubt, however, that for your Go-Bag or to put in your car in case you have to evacuate, a supply of freeze-dried foods are the best choice.

Option 2: Stocking Up From the Supermarket

Pros:

☑ You can spread the cost out over a long period of time if you can't afford a big amount up front.

☑ Supermarket food (cans, small packages, etc.) is easier to hide from the Food Police. My house is full of food but you can't see any of it—except what's in the cupboards for daily use—when you walk in. It would certainly be found in an organized search, but at least I stand a chance of bluffing the Food Police and holding onto my "hoard".

Cons:

☑ It will take quite a long time to stock everything you need.

☑ It won't stay edible for remotely as long as pre-packaged foods. Supermarket food lasts between six months to two years compared to up to 25 years for freeze-dried foods.

☑ Canned goods and dried foods have to be rotated out, eaten and replaced before they go bad. Further, canned goods will lose their nutritional value depending on the temperature of the storage place and the length of time they are stored.

☑ You have to repackage much of the supermarket food into sealed vacuum bags to preserve its shelf life. This is another chore to add to preparing and takes quite a bit of time—not to mention it is a messy project.

☑ If your goal is preparation for a long period of time (such as a year), your supermarket supplies will have to be supplemented by freeze-dried foods and purchases in bulk of items such as wheat, etc. to meet that goal.

How Much Food Do You Need?

Before you begin to shop, you need to have an idea of how much you will need to meet your family's food requirements for the period of time you have selected.

Matthew Stein, in his book *When Technology Fails*, helps you calculate your family's needs in bulk-food quantities. Based on the amount one average adult male needs for one year (and then adjusted for women and children), you can use the **Bulk Food Calculation Worksheet** (Appendix A) to calculate your family's food needs. The Worksheet has instructions for completion and Matt Stein's book, *When Technology Fails*, contains more information for your reference (pp 55 and 56).

You can use your estimates as a general guide for how much food you need to acquire, as well as a benchmark for how well you are progressing, whether the food is acquired in bulk or in smaller increments.

Choosing Your Food Purchase Strategy

It would be wise to investigate freeze-dried food and check out the prices before you start shopping. If your budget can't stretch that far, then proceed to the supermarket option. However, while researching freeze-dried foods, you should familiarize yourself with their offerings, which will be helpful later when supplementing your supermarket purchases.

What You Need to Know About Freeze-Dried Food

There are many businesses on the Internet that specialize in this type of food. Among them are:

- ☑ Solutions From Science, www.foodshortagesolutions.com
- ☑ Emergency Essentials, www.beprepared.com
- ☑ Survival Warehouse, http://www.survival-warehouse.com.
- ☑ The Ready House, http://www.thereadystore.com.
- ☑ E-Foods, http://www.efoodsdirect.com.
- ☑ Food Insurance, http://www.foodinsurance.com.

There are many others, but the above businesses are a good start.

Most of these businesses sell the food in units such as 7 days, 14 days, one month, and a one- year supply and above. Freeze-dried foods come in two basic ways:

- ☑ <u>Individual packages of one entrée,</u> such as chicken teriyaki with rice, beef stroganoff or turkey tetrazzini. The entire dinner is in one package and you don't need to do anything except add some water to make it edible.

- ☑ <u>Bulk cans and pails</u> that contain individual vegetable, fruits, eggs, and meat items in various sizes. You can also buy cans of the entrées, such as a whole can of beef stroganoff. Then you use only as much as you wish at one time.

The Food Insurance website offers a handy calculating tool for determining which package you should buy. You enter the number of adults and children you wish to feed in the boxes in the calculator, and then choose one of their packages. It will tell you the length of time that particular package will feed your family. You can use this calculator at http://www.foodinsurance.com/food_insurance/how_much_do_i_need.php. It only calculates for their products, but it will give you an idea of the amount of food a family eats in a given period of time.

I guarantee that it will surprise you. For instance, two adults and two children will have enough food for 211 days (about seven months) at three meals per day with their 1896 package. Regarding the storage issue, this package contains 29 boxes, each 13" x 13" x 7.25", and weighs 406 lbs. It costs over $5,000 plus shipping. But at the time of this writing (12/2010) you do get a FREE Drink Mix Combo and emergency kit!

The Freeze-Drying Process

The fresh or cooked food is first flash frozen. Then the flash-frozen food is put into a vacuum chamber where about 98% of the food's moisture is drawn off by evaporating the ice at temperatures as low as -50°F. Then it is sealed in moisture-and-oxygen-proof packaging. When it is opened and the water is replaced, the proponents of freeze-dried foods insist that the food regains its original fresh flavor, aroma, texture, appearance, and nutritional value. The package can be stored at room temperature and can last for up to 25 years. The freeze-drying process allows these food dealers to offers items like fruits, vegetables, juices, meat, dairy, eggs and even ice cream!! On a restricted or rationed diet, a five-pound tin of freeze-dried strawberries could be a real treat.

What You Need to Know About Shopping at the Supermarket

There are three major considerations when stocking large amounts of food long-term from the grocery store:

☑ Deciding what to buy and where to get it the least expensively
☑ Preserving and storing it
☑ Rotating it out and using it before it is unfit to eat

Where to Shop

☑ <u>Health/Organic food stores</u>: These are not usually economical or particularly useful for long-term food purchases, unless you are looking for interesting accents or tastes to spice up your core food stock. Regular supermarkets have much more variety of basic food stuffs at much better prices.

☑ <u>Local farmer or ethnic food markets</u>: The ones that cater to the wholesale restaurant trade carry larger and more economical units of rice, flour, salt, pepper, olive oil, noodles, etc.

A farmers market is a wonderful and fascinating place in which to shop. I have spent hours wandering up and down the aisles marveling at food tastes from around the world.

☑ Sam's Club, Costco, etc. If you are not a member of one of these outlets, you should check it out with your food and supplies lists in hand before joining and paying the fee. Make sure that they have enough of the items you need to make joining it cost effective.

☑ Nutrition/Herb Store: These stores sell dried herbs, sprout seeds, vitamins, holistic remedies and other useful items that are impossible to find elsewhere. If there is no such store in your area, there are many on the Internet. My experience is that the items carried in these stores are usually quite expensive. The wisest thing to do is make note of the supplements or food items you might be interested in, and then shop around on the Internet for lower prices. You will have to weigh your savings against added shipping costs, but if it comes out about even, then you will feel comfortable buying it from the local store.

☑ Farmers Supply Stores or Co-ops. If you can, try find a local farmers supply store or co-op within a reasonable distance. This may be difficult in a large urban area, as it usually ends up requiring long drives "to the country," or to small rural towns on the outskirts of the city. However, a farmers supply store is a good place to purchase seeds of all types, including cereals for making bread or growing wheat. Keep in mind that seeds are available on geographical basis and according to the dictates of Mother Nature. If it was a bad winter for wheat, then it's going to be hard to get locally. If you intend to shop locally, you must plan your acquisition and stocking schedule accordingly. However, you can order anything you want from the Internet at any time. There will be significant shipping costs however, as there is usually a lot of weight involved in shipping these types of items.

How To Shop for Food

You should keep your **Food Shopping List** with you at all times so you can take advantage of sales and promotions, especially 2-for-1 sales. When possible, purchase the store brands which are always cheaper.

TIP:

If you regard coffee as a basic food group and can't get your eyes open in the morning without it, then you should purchase as many large vacuum-packed cans of it as you can afford. Sealed glass jars are acceptable, but try not to buy coffee in plastic cans as your will have to re-package it for long-term storage. You may have to set aside your preference for the "ethically sourced" full-bodied Malaysian bean that is grown and gently hand-picked (come with me little bean, would you like a chair, slippers, a bottle of Perrier, anything?) on one hillside, in one island in Indonesia, which offers a rare bouquet and perfect smoothness—but you'll get over that very fast if there is no coffee available anywhere at any price. And don't forget to buy the non-electric percolator to make it with when the power is off. The best part is that extra coffee—if you can bear to part with it—will be a wonderful barter item. Imagine what people (who haven't had a cup of real coffee, Indonesian or otherwise, in six months) will trade you for an ounce of that precious and rare stuff!!! Coffee is one of the items (like soap) that will be priceless in a barter world. If you can find and purchase bulk amounts of whole coffee beans, they will store better and last longer than ground coffee.

Before your begin shopping, you should think carefully about your objective. You want to provide a <u>variety</u> of meals with <u>nutritional</u> <u>value</u> that will <u>fill your stomach</u>. The key is "mixing and matching." Your goal is to be able to make thick soups and stews with meat or vegetable stock and filled with vegetables or legumes (beans and peas), or dishes built around pasta, rice, noodles, etc. that will provide carbohydrates for energy, and nutrition from vegetables and other ingredients. Freeze-dried dairy products, meats, and fruits can be added to ensure variety, taste, and nutrition.

Therefore, you should build your food stock as follows:

☑ Buy as large an amount as you can of basic dried staples such as white rice. A 20-lb. bag of white rice will feed a small family for weeks. It is filling and can be combined with other foods in a virtually infinite way. Buy lots of rice. You might get bored with rice-based dinners, but you won't starve. White rice is the best to buy for long-term storage. Brown and exotic rice may be interesting to look at and smell nice, but they have oils that will turn rancid and ruin the rice in a much shorter time than white rice. White rice, properly sealed, will last for years.

TIP:
Rice is amazing! When I was living in Poland one summer, I went to a little café every day that served a rice dish with peas in an egg sauce. It was delicious, cost about $1, provided two meals, and filled me for most of the day. I have never been able to duplicate it exactly here, even though it is simple as pie to make. Using a few cups of rice, some real or powdered eggs, and a can of peas, you have an OTG meal that is both nutritious and filling.

☑ Noodles and beans serve the same function as rice. In comparison to their weight and the space they take up, they bulk up when cooked and are very nutritious. Get a lot of noodles and all kinds of beans. Some bean soups come pre-mixed which makes your cooking job easier, especially when it has become a chore if there is no electricity. You usually soak the bean mix overnight, then toss the whole thing into a pot with water, add a meat or vegetable flavoring if you wish, simmer for several hours, and you have a nutritious soup meal that will feed a small family for several meals.

☑ Buy things like dried soups, noodles, potatoes, sauces, onions, powdered milk, cereals, popcorn, and crackers in the largest sizes you can get.

TIP:
When buying dried staples, check your local farmers market or restaurant supply stores as you will be able to get larger amounts and more variety of these items at a better price than at the supermarket.

☑ Buy canned goods to supplement a basic rice or noodle concoction including vegetables, canned potatoes, fruits, canned meats, and canned fish. Don't forget peanut butter and jelly.

☑ Buy accent foods such as salt, pepper, sugar, herbs, and spices. Items like a big can of wonton soup mix could make a different tasting base for soups when you get tired of chicken, beef or vegetable.

☑ Buy breakfast bars, nuts, etc. to provide little treats every now and then.

If possible, you should also purchase a few cans of freeze-dried dairy, meat, fruit, or vegetable products to round out your diet and provide variety. You can buy them in bulk in cans of various sizes.

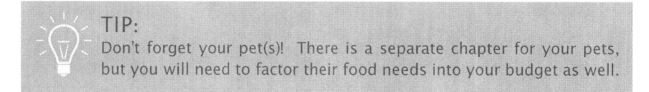

TIP:
Don't forget your pet(s)! There is a separate chapter for your pets, but you will need to factor their food needs into your budget as well.

What you actually purchase is, of course, dependent on your family's tastes, ethnic considerations, and issues with food. For instance, perhaps someone can't eat peanut butter or dairy products. Only you know what "mixes-and-matches" your family will eat. A suggested **Food Shopping List** is provided later in this chapter, but you will want to add or subtract to it for your family's tastes and needs.

Take a Stroll Around Your Supermarket

I hate food shopping and budget is always an issue. I usually go into a supermarket with a list, buzz around, get just what I need, and get out like my tail is on fire. If you are the same, you should consider slowing down on your next trip and taking a few moments to consider what the supermarket would look like in an OTG world. For instance, forget that the meat, bread, produce, fish, dairy, and frozen foods sections exist because in the OTG world (and perhaps on occasions in the FEND world or after a sudden disaster), those shelves, bins, and freezer compartments will be empty. You can skip the pop, wine, candy, and potato chips aisle too.

Focus on the canned goods (including meats), pastas, and the dried food aisles. That actually leaves about three aisles worth of stuff in the whole store. Take a little time and poke around. Finger things you don't normally look at or buy, and mentally mix and match items. A can of Chicken A La King with rice can make a whole dinner. Cans of tuna go with noodles of all types. Pre-mixed dried soups in sealed packages, although more expensive than canned soups, will make a large pot of thick delicious soup. Dried potato soups in vacuum packs are especially rich and nutritious, and you might have a hard time getting potatoes any other way without growing your own. Pre-mixed bean soups are a very good buy. Beef and chicken broths will enrich a plain soup made of odds and ends. Fruit in a can will make a good dessert or snack.

Taking a little time to browse will trigger your imagination. You'll be glad you did when your family says, "Rice again?" and you can answer, "Well, actually, yes. But it's got peanut butter, peas and raisins in it. Mmmmm, tasty."

Storing Your Food

If you bought your food pre-packaged, all you have to do is find a cool, dry place to keep it. But if you are buying it from the supermarket, you must repackage it yourself so it lasts longer. There are two basic steps to food storage preparation:

☑ You should note the month and year of purchase on your canned goods with a marker. Canned goods also carry a "best if eaten by" date stamp. Your target time for rotating out foods starts with the purchase date and ends with the "best if eaten by" date stamp. If the "best eaten by" date has passed, the food MUST be tossed out. Botulism is a very bad deal and doubly so if in a FEND or OTG situation. If any can is damaged, rusted, or bulging, it must be tossed out. It is not worth your life.

TIP:
Holly Drennan Deyo's *Dare to Prepare!* (3rd edition) deals in depth with food selection and storage matters. You can get it at: www.daretoprepare.com. Click on the picture of the book and it will take you to the Table of Contents and ordering information. It costs $58 plus shipping. This book is over 600 pages long and is an excellent reference book for all OTG survival skills.

☑ Any food item that is not vacuum sealed or canned must be re-packaged with a Seal-A-Meal or similar unit. With these units, you cut a roll of plastic to the size of bag you want, put one of the open ends in the sealer and melt it shut. Use the bag that creates to put your food product in, and then seal the other end in the unit. The unit sucks all of the air out of the plastic pouch and seals it. The package gets hard as a rock. If it does not, it is not properly sealed and you should start again.

TIP:
The Seal-A-Meal or similar unit is available at any department store or from the Internet. It should cost about $70. Make sure you get a sealing unit with a cutting edge inside it so you can cut the plastic rolls clean and straight. Some units offer a vacuum tube attachment that you can use to seal food into special plastic bowls that is handy. You will also need a supply of plastic rolls or pre-cut bags to use with it. The bags aren't cheap, and I presume this is where they make their real money. You can buy boxes of pre-cut bags, but buying it by the roll is more economical and lets you create the size of bags you want for each item.

What Foods to Seal

☑ Any food product in a plastic bag (even if it is sealed), a paper sack, cardboard box, or even a plastic can, must be re-packaged for long-term storage. Food in foil packages may be left for awhile, but if they are intended to be kept for over a year, you should also seal them. Be sure to keep the preparation instructions from the package. You can cut it out and put it in the bag with the food, or keep it in a central place for reference later.

TIP:

The Seal-A-Meal doesn't work properly with hard, pointy food items such as noodles or macaroni. The noodles prick small holes in the bag as the air is sucked out, and the bag doesn't seal. I wasted a lot of bags this way until I figured out it was hopeless and gave up. Re-package your noodles in plastic baggies and push as much air out of them as you can. Also, unless you like food surprises, be sure you identify your bags by putting the plastic package in with the item or using a labeling machine. It is very hard to tell pancake mix from white corn meal when it is in brick form. After you have sealed the bags, let them sit for a few hours before hiding them because sometimes the bags slowly leak. It takes a while for you to see that the bag has gotten all floppy and therefore isn't sealed.

Food Storage for Bulk Supplies

It gets a little more complicated when storing bulk foods such as wheat, corn, rice, etc. In these cases, for large quantities, the Seal-A-Meal is not the answer. You will need:

☑ Large buckets that tightly seal

☑ Some method of inhibiting the oxygen in the container to discourage bugs

To discourage bugs you can get some oxygen absorption packets or use dry ice. The oxygen absorption packets can be purchased through Amazon. Dry ice requires more care and some skill. You can find instructions for handling dry ice in Matthew Stein's book, *When Technology Fails*. Another book that deals with stockpiling food and food storage issues is:

☑ *How to Survive The End of the World As We Know It: Tactics, Techniques, and Technologies for Uncertain Times* by James Wesley, Rawles. (Yes, that is how he spells his name.) You can get it on Amazon.

Hiding Your Food

However you obtain your food, you should hide it, keeping only your daily supply in the kitchen cupboards. All indicators point to the strong possibility that in a food crisis, the PTB (Powers That Be) at the federal, state or local level may decide that all food stocks should be centralized and distributed by the government to those who need it.

Your goals in hiding food are:

- ☑ Not to have large amounts of food out in plain sight

- ☑ To make it so annoying and difficult to find, that the searchers don't want to spend the time and effort

I have food hidden all over my house. It is vacuum-sealed so it will not attract bugs and will keep as long as possible. It is hidden in, under, and behind every conceivable free space. You should, however, not keep canned goods (which degrade quickly in poor climatically-controlled conditions) in places such as an uninsulated attic or garage, or the outdoors.

TIP:
Sam Adam's *Hide Your Guns* offers useful strategies for hiding anything in your home, not just guns. You can get it at www.hideyourguns. com for $50 in audio or print form.

Unless you can afford to build, or have built, your own custom hiding place, here are a few strategies for hiding food:

- ☑ Be creative when looking for places where you can hide food. Any empty space—even inside furniture—is fair game. Try to find places that require a little extra effort to find. You can hide food behind one row of books but you run the risk that someone idly pulling down one book may expose the whole stash. Put your food behind two rows of books on a top shelf so pulling down one row of books for a quick look only nets the searcher another row of books. They may pull down the second row of books too, but maybe you'll get lucky.

☑ Store food either high or low when possible. Don't make it easy for the Food Police to expose it by idly poking around. Unless the searcher is very tall, they will not be able to see the items from above, and crawling around near the floor, yanking stuff out of dusty corners and off shelves, is wearying. Not replacing a dead light bulb in an area that doesn't endanger people might be a good idea too.

☑ Fill some boxes completely with household items such as seasonal clothing, children's toys, sheets and towels, household goods, books, etc. Label them clearly as "Winter Clothing," etc. Then fill other boxes with food on the bottom and household items on the top, and label them with the name of the household items that are on the top. If you are using old towels for camouflage, for instance, put two proper towels on top and then layer some food inside the folds of the third, fourth and then under the fifth one. Hopefully a searcher will lift the top towels, see more towels, and give up.

☑ When you pile them up, put the boxes filled with actual household items in them in the front and on top of the pile. Two or three rows of boxes from the top, or behind the front row of properly labeled boxes, you place the boxes filled with half food and half household items. A searcher, who pulls down a box (or two or three), opens them up and sees winter clothes and toys, might just give up. Tape them up so it's even more annoying to have to open them.

☑ You should start keeping boxes or containers that are not marked with giveaway labels for survival supplies. Keep the box the coffee maker or the juicer came in, or bring home boxes from the office supply place at work. Throw all these empty boxes on top of the pile. Keep the Styrofoam and peanuts too, just to make it messier for them to poke through.

☑ Don't fill any one box to the top with food unless you can't help it. Although it might say "Winter Clothes," when it's lifted and it's as heavy as an anvil, it's a dead giveaway. Put that one right at the bottom and maybe they won't bother to lift it or move it.

☑ You can store a pile of winter blankets and slip the food between the folds. Put the blankets inside a big plastic bag so it can be lifted intact and not spill the food. The searcher would have to pull out not only the sack, but will also have to pull everything out of the sack to find the food. Since the blankets can be clearly identified through the plastic, they may not mess with it. You can store some of the flatter items in the middle of rolled up rugs stood up against the wall. Secure the rug rolls shut with a LOT of tape.

☑ Do you have a stack of old jigsaw puzzle boxes the kids left behind years ago, and which all have pieces missing from them and you were going to throw out anyway? Put some light, flat food in several of them, tape them down so they don't move, and keep some of the pieces so the box rattles like it's full. Seal it with a lot of tape on the outside, and then stick the food puzzle boxes to the back of a pile of other stuff with the label "To the Next Rummage Sale" on them.

☑ If you do store some food items in the garage, put that old bike that needs a new chain, along with a bunch of old tools and bags of mulch for the garden, the garden hose that leaks, that box of stray hardware, doorknobs, cans of screws, and a bunch of that left-over brick you put around the garden beds, in front of or on top of them, and anything else you can find that will be annoying to move. Your goal is to make it disagreeable, hard—and maybe even apparently dangerous—for them to poke right to the back or to the bottom of boxes and bins. I realize that for neat people this is actually painful. But ask yourself if you would rather be neat or eat. The answer should be obvious.

☑ When storing food in closets, put the food all the way to the back and put a lot of miscellaneous, hard-to-move, unboxed individual items like fans or other household items on top of them. The more little individual stuff there is to move, the less anyone will want to do it. You can create little hidey holes with a few matching boards or peg board that would need to be removed to get to the food, but which look natural. Hang things on the peg board to make it harder to see through it and make it look used.

☑ Finally, don't store all one type of food in one place. If one place is found, perhaps another will be missed.

I really hate having to hide stuff. My whole life I have regularly cleaned out my possessions and kept only what I needed and used, giving the rest away or throwing it out. I actually like cleaning stuff out because it feels good to be neat and tidy. I do not enjoy my closets heaped up with the cat carrier teetering on top of the Mr. Coffee box with Styrofoam and plastic sticking out of it, which is balanced on top of the big plastic bin of empty jars, all of which wobbles on that old broken stereo and speakers that sits on the box that contains six cans of freeze-dried food that will feed me for six months and which is labeled "Winter Clothes" and has two pairs of old jeans in the top of it.

I hope I have given you some good ideas that you can use to apply to your own home. Make hiding stuff into an art form. This method of hiding is obviously not foolproof, but it is your only defense against confiscation without building a custom hiding place. A dedicated searcher will throw all the books on the floor, toss all boxes out of the closets, and tear the garage apart. But maybe you'll get lucky and they'll have had a long day of stealing other people's stuff and just want to go home. They may give up on you as an eccentric person hopelessly afflicted with "packratitis" whose closets clearly indicate that you couldn't organize a birthday party, much less prepare for the end of the world.

There is one serious problem with this disorganized type of hiding. With supermarket food, you have to rotate it out and eat it. I am already feeling the effects of this because I have to search a lot of places for the stuff I need to rotate out now. And it's not easy to get to either—by design. This is unfortunate, but unavoidable, if you don't have a deep underground bunker hidden in the back yard where it can all be put neatly on shelves. It might help to keep similarly timed purchases more or less together. Keep a cryptic list with dates and storage locations on it. In the event of a search, if there is time, any lists should be quickly hidden or destroyed. There is nothing like a map to the treasure sitting right out on the kitchen counter to make life easy for the PTB.

Alternate Food Strategies: Making Your Own Food

Anything you've bought from the supermarket or in freeze-dried form will eventually run out if the crisis lasts long enough. For the FEND and OTG tracks, you should be thinking about:

- ☑ How to supplement the food you have to make it last longer
- ☑ How to shift entirely off commercial food if it appears that the crisis will last for years

Fortunately, there are several things you can do to become more independent of commercial food sources now, supplement your dwindling food stock during hard times, and to which you can then shift over to if the crisis period is indeterminate and all your stored food runs out.

TIP:
You can learn to can and dehydrate your own food with a DVD set that has a video course on canning and an introduction to dehydrating fruits, vegetables, and meats. You can purchase this course at www.foodshortageusa.com for $40.

Food Dehydration

You can dehydrate many common foods (for instance your garden crops) to preserve them for up to a year. Dehydration is the process of removing water from food, which inhibits the growth of micro-organisms and bacteria. It is easy to do and does not necessarily need any expensive equipment. If done properly, the food is tasty, nutritious, lightweight, and lasts much longer..

You can dry fruits, vegetables, meats, fish, and herbs. The length of time it takes is dependent on the water and sugar content in the food, the size of the food piece, and the air circulation, humidity, and air temperature inside the dehydrator. Some foods should be pre-treated for the best results, to keep them from turning brown and losing vitamins A and C.

TIP:
There are many methods of pre-treatment. Some of the simpler methods including using lemon juice, fruit juice, or fruit juice concentrates. For a complete discussion of pre-treating, including sulphuring, an excellent book is *How To Dry Foods: The Most Complete Guide to Drying Foods at Home* by Deanna DeLong. You can get it at Amazon. There is also a lot of information on drying food on the Internet.

Dehydration does slightly affect the nutritional value of food. For instance, some vitamin C is lost during the drying process. However, the caloric value, the fiber, and carbohydrate content all remain the same.

If you want to dehydrate foods for use in your daily life, or to store up for or supplement a FEND situation, you can:

- ☑ Build your own dehydrator (plans are available all over the Internet)
- ☑ Use your own oven (if the utilities are working)
- ☑ Buy a non-electric dehydrator
- ☑ Buy an electric dehydrator

If you wish to purchase a simple but effective natural food dehydrator, I recommend the unit from Food Pantrie. It has five perforated shelves that slide into a hanging unit which is surrounded by a gauze fabric. You can hang the entire unit inside or outside. The shelves are dishwasher safe, and it folds down to about 3 inches high by 15 inches square. You can also grow sprouts and wheatgrass in it in far more volume than a countertop sprouter. Five shelves give a fair amount of space, but you may want to purchase more than one if you really want to dry a lot of food continuously. You can purchase the Food Pantrie at Amazon for about $45.

An electric food dehydrator is faster than the natural method. There are several things to look for in a quality food dehydrator:

- ☑ It should have at least 750 watts of drying power. The higher the wattage, the faster the food dries.

- ☑ An air flow system that forces heated air up or down the exterior of the chamber and then horizontally across each individual tray. This means you do not need to rotate the trays for even drying.

- ☑ An adjustable thermostat so you can dry different foods at different temperatures. For instance, meats and fish should be dried at 145°F and above; fruits and vegetables, between 130°F to 140°F.

- ☑ A digital programmable timer for up to 48 hours is nice, but optional.

- ☑ An opaque exterior so the food retains most of its nutrients and vitamins.

- ☑ It should be expandable—that is, you can add additional trays for more volume.

A unit such as described above can dry fruit and beef in hours, not days.

TIP:
You can get inexpensive dehydrators such as the Ronco FD 1005 5-Tray Electric unit for about $40, but it has only 125 watts of power and can take up to three days to the do the same drying as its more powerful counterparts do in a few hours. In addition, these units are cheaply made and do not last. You would do better to just get the Food Pantrie with the same money.

I recommend the Nesco American Harvest FD-1018P Dehydrator Kit. It is a countertop unit that has 1,000 watts of power, a bottom fan, and an adjustable thermost. I own this product and it is excellent. It comes with eight trays (and can be expanded to 30) and all the trays have screens. Eight fruit roll sheets are also included. It does hum relatively loudly when running and puts out a fair amount of heat, so you should set it away from other items on your counter. After running for five or six hours, it actually contributes to the general warmth of the kitchen. It is 18 inches in diameter by 16 inches high with all eight trays stacked up. You can buy additional trays for $15 for two trays. It comes with an instruction and recipe book. You can get it from Amazon for $150. You can also make beef jerky with the unit but you will need to purchase the Nesco BJX-5 American Harvest Jumbo Jerky Works Kit for $15.

You shouldn't wait for an emergency to dehydrate fruit and vegetables. They make wonderful snacks anytime. You can make thin, crispy apple chips or strawberry crunchies in just a few hours. It is, however, a bit unnerving at first to dry a whole quart of strawberries and put the result in a small peanut butter jar, or fill all the trays with apple slices and get two stuffed sandwich baggies out of it. You can easily return the dehydrated item back to its original state by putting it in water and voila! fifteen minutes later it's b-a-a-a-c-k!

TIP:
You can learn to can and dehydrate your own food with a DVD set that has a video course on canning and an introduction to dehydrating fruits, vegetables, and meats. You can purchase this course at www.foodshortageusa.com for $40.

Canning

Our elders canned because they didn't have refrigerators—and you may not either in a FEND or OTG situation. I clearly remember watching my grandmother canning over a steaming, old fashioned stove. (Yes, I'm that old.) She kept the jars in a cool dark place in the cellar. She would regularly surface from there with a jar of the sweetest peaches and raspberry jams I've ever tasted. I can still hear the little pop the vacuum top made when she pried it off. Nothing in modern cans even touches the taste of what came out of those jars.

Canning is not hard, but you do have to be careful to do it right so your canned food doesn't get infected with botulism. Only fruits can be processed in a boiling bath water canner; you will need pressure canning equipment for all other foods.

TIP:
DO NOT confuse a pressure canner with a pressure cooker. They are not the same. The pressure cooker is not as reliable and is not recommended.

You will need:

☑ A 16- to 22-quart pressure canner. While some people like a canner with a weighted gauge to measure the pressure, a dial gauge is more accurate when it comes to adjusting pressure for altitudes and for keeping the pressure consistent in the canner. All in all, it depends on what type of equipment you get used to when canning (your stove also has an effect on the canning process), and the results you get with the end product. Your canner should also have a rack for sitting the jars on.

☑ Canning tongs or a jar lifter (to get the jars out of the water) and a funnel. You can buy sets of canning tools and do not have to buy them all individually.

☑ A supply of glass canning jars. These are available in many sizes and mouth widths. You will need the special two-piece lids which are composed of a screw ring and a rubber-seal lid. You can use the screw rings again but not the sealing lid, so get extra for the sizes of jars you have bought.

TIP:
In this case you should NOT use the glass jars you have been saving as they are not made for the high temperatures and pressures of canning. The old glass jars with bailed-wire seals and rubber rings are also not recommended.

You should study canning techniques carefully before you begin because getting botulism in FEND or OTG is very bad. Two excellent resources are:

☑ *The Big Book of Preserving the Harvest: 150 Recipes for Freezing, Canning, Drying, and Pickling Fruits and Vegetables* by Carol W. Costenbader.

☑ *Stocking Up: The Classic Preserving Guide* by Carol Hupping

You can also invest in a DVD course on canning and dehydrating food called *Food Storage Secrets* from www.foodshortageusa.com. It costs $40.

A pressure canner isn't hard to find, although they are not as common as pressure cookers. They are, of course, offered on Amazon, ranging in price from $80 to $200. Walmart.com also carries pressure canners for a reasonable price, and you can even find new ones offered on eBay. You can also find them in some farmers markets. But remember: You want a <u>pressure canner</u> not just a <u>pressure cooker</u>.

Sprouts and Sprouting

Sprouts are seeds that you grow into small seedlings and then eat (both the seed and the small sprout). They are one of the most concentrated sources of vitamins, minerals, enzymes, and amino acids (protein) known, and they rival red meat and garden produce in nutritional value. This will be important on a FEND or OTG diet.

You don't plant the seeds in soil outside; rather, they are grown indoors in a container. The seeds are soaked in water for a few hours and then kept moist, and they sprout into seedlings. In a few days, you have a delicious and nutritious food or supplement to your food. You can use them in nearly everything—to make sandwiches crunchier, in salads, soups, or whatever else your imagination can think up. Nearly every seed (beans, grains, and nuts included) can be sprouted, but some, such as alfalfa, are more common and inexpensive than others. One pound of alfalfa seeds results in about seven pounds of alfalfa sprouts. Mung beans enjoy a ten-fold increase in volume.

To sprout seeds you can:

- ☑ Use your own jar with cheesecloth fastened over the top with a string or rubber band. The jars can also be covered with a little plastic mesh cap so you can rinse them with fresh water and then drain it out. This is the least expensive way to grow sprouts if you have the jars, costing only a few dollars for the caps.

- ☑ Buy a counter top sprouter, of which there are many different designs (multiple trays, round, square, etc.) These smaller sprouters don't make many sprouts at one time (about what one person could eat in a day or two), so you may need to purchase a larger unit or several small ones so you can provide enough sprouts for everyone in your family.

The more common sprouts are alfalfa, mung beans, and lentils. But radish, green peas, garbanzo beans, red clover, broccoli, chick peas, sunflower, sesame, soy, wheat seeds, and many others can also be sprouted. Seeds are also available in various mixes for salads and other uses. Some of them, such a broccoli, are relatively expensive, so, if you are on a budget, build your sprout stocks with alfalfa, mung beans, and lentils as they are common and inexpensive. You can add some of the more exotic seeds like radish or broccoli in small amounts as a treat.

To start sprouting, you need:

- ☑ Some sort of sprouting container: a jar with cheesecloth or plastic meshed lid, a countertop sprouter, or a large tray(s) unit

- ☑ Sprouts and water

You do NOT need a green thumb. It's hard to keep these things from growing almost in front of your eyes. About all you can do to ruin sprouts is to keep them too wet so they get moldy, or let them get too dry where they wither, but that's about it.

The Internet has many sources for sprouts seeds and sprouting equipment. The company I order the most sprouts from is Handy Pantry Sprouting, www.handypantry.com/, but there are many others. And for food purists Handy Pantry's seeds are organic! You can get them in mixes or by individual seed in a variety of sizes.

TIP:
You can also get common sprout seeds such as mung and soy beans from the farmers market because they are widely used in Asian cooking. Large packages of these beans can be bought very inexpensively. You can get the more unusual seeds from the Internet sprouting places. Amazon also has basic sprouting seeds like alfalfa by the pound.

Handy Pantry carries starter sprouting kits with a selection of seeds. Their kit comes in a 5-gallon bucket that can be resealed (yes, a bucket too!!!) and has 16 pounds of a variety of organic sprouts made up of 9 different seeds and seed mixes. You also get a countertop sprouter and three plastic lids for sprouting in glass jars. The cost is $130 but is actually quite cost effective considering the type and amount of the seeds they put in there. There are other starter kits available as well from other dealers, some less expensive.

Solutions From Science also offers a larger sprouting kit that comes with 55 pounds of sprouting seeds (10 different varieties that include alfalfa, radish, broccoli, mung bean, wheat, pea, fenugreek, garbanzo, green lentils, and black-eyed peas) and all the equipment you need to begin sprouting today. You can find their kit at http://survivalsproutbank.com/.

You can buy a countertop sprouter ($10 to $20) from the Internet and get some basic seeds (lentils, mung, and alfalfa) from Amazon or the supermarket. (Split peas or lentils from the supermarket will not sprout.) Amazon also carries a whole variety of sprouters for every taste, as well as lids and seeds. Just make sure that the sprouter you buy will hold tiny seeds in at least one of the trays.

And, yes, you will have to break out the Seal-a-Meal and seal up any sprouts seeds that are not already vacuum-packed until you are ready to use them.

TIP:
You shouldn't sprout garden seeds because they may have been treated with chemicals.

Amazon also has plenty of books on growing spouts. *The Sprouting Book: How to Grow and Use Sprouts to Maximize Your Health and Vitality* by Ann Wigmore is a good one, but there are many others from which to choose.

Finally, if you want to do what amounts to industrial-strength sprouting, you can invest in the Sproutman Wheatgrass Grower from . . . you guessed it, Amazon, or www.sproutman.com. This is a large three-tray unit that is designed for sprouting wheatgrass seeds, but it will sprout the larger seeds and beans as well. You could feed an army from one tray (never mind three) of this unit. It costs $100. It will be covered in more detail in the Wheatgrass section, so check there for details.

TIP:
Sprout growing as a small home business for income or barter is not a bad idea to consider if we are all OTG.

Don't wait for a catastrophe to grow sprouts. They are wonderful right now. They are surprisingly crunchy and tasty, and make a wonderful snack food instead of potato chips or other snacks.

Growing and Juicing Wheatgrass

Wheatgrass is another form of sprouting but with a different final result, and which requires more expensive equipment. Wheatgrass berries are wheat seeds that you sprout until the grass is several inches high. It looks just like your lawn, but with no weeds and probably greener.

Wheat grass has the same benefits as sprouts—that is, it contains vitamins, minerals, chlorophyll, and enzymes. The drink is bright green and tastes like, um, well . . . vaguely sweet grass. Unusual. I personally don't care for it all that much, certainly not to drink straight down. Fortunately, you can mix it with fruit or vegetable drinks. It's the new trendy thing in juice bars. Finally, you're on the cutting edge instead of ten years behind!

Before you start, you may wish to invest in a book on growing wheatgrass and its benefits. Ann Wigmore's, *The Wheatgrass Book: How to Grow and Use Wheatgrass to Maximize you Health and Vitality* is a good one, but there are others on Amazon.

To grow wheat grass you will need:

- ☑ Wheat grass seeds
- ☑ Wheat grass seed growing trays
- ☑ An electric and/or non-electric juicer that can specifically juice wheatgrass

You need larger trays to grow wheat grass because you need a lot of it to make one glass of juice. Grass, unlike peaches or apples, is just not that juicy. The Sproutman Wheatgrass Grower has three large trays with lids that fit into a plastic frame. It can be broken down for storage, much like those stackable plastic office storage units. You can get it at (yes) Amazon or www.sproutman.com for $100. The good part about it is, you can also use it to grow larger batches of sprout seeds too.

It's not hard to grow wheat seeds: you soak them for several hours, sprinkle them on the grid inside the tray, keep them covered for awhile, then let the light in and let the grass grow to about 7 or 8 inches high. Then you mow it with scissors. However, unlike a cow, which has a stomach with four parts and re-chews the grasses she eats, humans cannot eat grass or wheatgrass because our stomachs are not built to digest it properly. You have to juice the grass into a drink.

A Word on Juicers

Juicers can be a little confusing. Department stores and specialty stores have shelves full of them touting all the bells and whistles, telling you how healthy you're going be at age 105 if you just buy their product and use it every day. You can easily get lost, so here's a little primer.

You should look for the following features:

1. Ease of cleaning
2. Noise level
3. Speed of juicing
4. Types of food stuffs you will be processing.

There are several basic types of juicers:

☑ **Centrifugal Juicers:** A grater or shredder disc at the bottom of the basket revolves at high speed like a washing machine on the spin cycle and pulps the food stuff. You push the food in the top through a little chute. Some of these juicers eject the pulp while others keep it inside, making it necessary to clean them out at intervals before you can continue juicing. Centrifugal juicers are good for juicing most fruits and vegetables.

☑ **Masticating Juicers:** This type first grates, then chews the pulp to further extract the juice, and finally, mechanically squeezes or presses the pulp to get the remaining juice out. Some of these machines are so powerful that they can juice leafy vegetables and make foods such as raw applesauce, tomato sauce, baby food, and peanut butter.

☑ **Auger Juicers (Single or Dual Stage):** These types of juicers use an auger (big screw) that crushes the food stuff into the walls or screen of the juicer, extracting the juice. These are often sold for juicing wheat grass. Some can do vegetables as well, but they are not good for fruit as they usually leave a lot of pulp in the juice.

☑ **Twin Gear Press:** These machines have two gears that basically press the juice out of the food. These machines are good for juicing vegetables, and can juice wheatgrass as well.

So you can see what you are up against. Fortunately, there is one juicer—the Hurom HU-100—that works for both wheat grass and other foods. You can find out more about this juicer in this section.

In addition to the wheat grass tray and lots of wheat seeds, you need a good electric juicer and/or a manual juicer to be able to use your wheat grass. If you already have a good electric juicer that can handle wheatgrass, then it makes sense to give growing wheat grass a try. If you do not already own a juicer, there is one juicer that works both with wheat grass and other foods as well. The Hurom Slow Juicer HU-100 is a single-auger juicer with a crushing function. This juicer squeezes the material rather than grinds it, allowing the juice to maintain its color, taste, nutrients, and vitamins. The juicer comes with fine and coarse screens, pulp extraction plugs, a self-cleaning screen holder, two 50-ounce juicing cups, a tamper, a brush, and an instruction manual. It measures approximately 9-3/4 inches long by 6-3/4 inches wide by 15-3/4 inches high and has a ten-year warranty.

You can get a Hurom Juicer HU-100 at Amazon for $360. I think it is the finest juicer on the market. It will process fruits, vegetables, leafy greens, soy, and wheatgrass. What's left of the wheat grass is just a dried green husk.

Of course, the Hurom Slow Juicer will only work if there is electricity, so for OTG you need a manual juicer. I have one and frankly, it does a terrible job. It is a mess-intensive, low-production, high-energy means of getting only a dribble out of your very selfishly non-juicy wheat grass. So wheat grass in the OTG world is not very practical. You can, however, get wheat grass powder, which makes a whole lot more sense in OTG, although it is less beneficial that fresh wheat grass. You can get it at Amazon and it's not that expensive.

So my final recommendation on growing and juicing wheatgrass is:

☑ If you are on a budget and do not already have an electric juicer of any kind, put your money and energy into setting up a sprouts production operation. Sprouting is a lower-cost, less work-intensive approach that produces a lot more benefits. You can purchase small countertop sprouters, or the Sproutman if you want more volume.

☑ If you already have a juicer that can handle wheat grass, then go ahead and try it. Buy some wheat seeds and the Sproutman and knock yourself out.

☑ If you are looking for an excuse to buy a good electric juicer, then growing wheat grass gives you as good a reason as any. Get the Hurom HU-100 if you can because it is fabulous for wheat grass smashing.

☑ You will more than likely have to order your wheat seeds from the Internet, unless you can find a local bulk supply.

They are costly to ship because they are heavy. However, you should probably invest in some wheat seeds anyway. The same wheat seeds you use to grow wheat grass can also be ground to make bread or even plant in the garden, if you wish. See the "Speaking of Wheat" section that is next for more information.

If all this seems like too much trouble and expense, and you still want to try it, get some wheat grass powder from Amazon. Let the purists spend hundreds of dollars to get a little cup of green liquid grass; you just add water.

Speaking of Wheat: Did Someone Say Bread?

I don't know about you, but I think a world without bread isn't worth living in. If you want bread and bread products in a FEND or OTG world, you will have to plan ahead. I can remember my grandmother baking bread and the delicious smell it made as it came out of the oven, hot and soft. As it cooled on the table for dinner, the aroma drove me mad, and I kept stealing pieces until I got yelled at to quit and wait for dinner. It was still warm and the butter melted on it. To this day, her bread is the best I have ever tasted.

If you are going to make delicious breads of your own, you will need:

- ☑ Wheat flour or whole wheat berries (seeds)
- ☑ Yeast (or be able to make it yourself)
- ☑ A grain mill if you are intending to grind your own wheat berries
- ☑ An oven

Buying an Oven for FEND or OTG

Obviously, you can make bread anytime in a bread machine or in your own oven, but if there are no utilities, what then? The answer is a solar (or sun) oven. The Solutions From Science's solar oven is perfect for OTG baking. It is a box lined with metal, with a glass lid and reflective wings that you spread out to catch the sun. It looks a little like the Lunar Landing Module (LEM). There is a thermometer inside that is easy to read. It collapses down into a square box-shaped unit.

You can bake anything in it and it will make two loaves of bread at a time. I tried it out this summer. I made one loaf of bread and to be fair, it took a little while. You won't be able to start an OTG bakery with this unit. However, it worked just fine and the bread was delicious.

You can use regular baking pans and it needs no other equipment except sunlight. You do need to fiddle with the reflective screens during the day to keep tracking the sun efficiently.

TIP:
Be very careful with the glass lid. Breaking it will ruin your unit and you could hurt yourself. It doesn't have any guards along the edges to make it sturdier, so be careful.

You can get the solar oven from Solutions From Science by going to their website www.bestsolaroven.com.

Grain Mills

If you intend to grind your own wheat seeds, then you will need a grain mill. Like juicers, there are many types of grain mills, each with their advantages and disadvantages. The differences lie in the method by which they grind the grain and whether they are electric or manual. Here is a short tutorial on the various types:

☑ **Impact Mills.** Sometimes called "micronizers," these units are generally made of a plastic exterior, weigh only a few pounds, and are relatively inexpensive. They do not "grind" grain. Instead the grain is fed into a series of rings of metal teeth. A spindle in the center of the cone of metal teeth circulates the grain at 28,000 revolutions per minute. The speed of the unit means that grain dust can get everywhere and the unit can overheat, so you have to monitor their use. Any foreign body (a small stone for instance) can damage the teeth. In addition, they are very loud. One reviewer described them as "whining and screaming," and likened it to being on an airport tarmac while a jet engine revs up. Their advantage is they make a very fine powder very quickly. Manufacturers have been working to mitigate the sound problem, and the GrainMaster WhisperMill and NutriMill include sound dampeners and other modifications that make them <u>somewhat</u> quieter. They do not generally offer a wide range of texture options (from coarse to fine), but do a fine powder very well.

☑ **Stone Mills:** In general, stone mills are heavier than micronizers (over 50 lbs.) and much bulkier. They also tend to cost more. The grain is ground between stones and you can only mill dry grains without problems.

"Wet" grains stick to the stones and clog up the unit, requiring cleaning and constant monitoring of the operation in case it overheats. On the other hand, they are durable and sturdy. The stones need to be adjusted and cleaned occasionally. Unlike the micronizers, they can produce different coarsenesses of grains for different uses. Stone mills can be purchased in high, intermediate, or slow speeds. High-speed stone mills are very noisy and dusty. You could supply a small bakery with their output, but they can get very hot and have to be watched during operation. The intermediate and slow-speed stone mills mitigate the dust and noise problem somewhat. A slow-speed stone mill can produce about ½ to 1 cup of flour per minute. This is perfectly adequate for family use.

☑ **Burr and Hand Mills.** Burr mills grind the grain between two metal pieces with raised cutting surfaces. You can get them in both manual and electric versions.

The purpose of this guide is to make it easy for you. Therefore, taking all of the above into account, the most economic and flexible unit is the Family Grain Mill from Pleasant Hill Grain in Nebraska (www.pleasanthillgrain.com under "Grain Mills.") This mill is unique. It can mill grains to any fineness, crack the grains and, with a flaker attachment, can even flake the berries into oatmeal. It is both electric and manual. The grain mill can be attached to its hand base for manual operation (it comes with the mill), or it can be assembled with the electric motor and used that way. You can also grind herbs and spices. It is quiet and easy to set up. This unit is ideal for moving from a FEND situation with electricity to an OTG world with no electricity, and is well-priced and sturdy.

TIP:
Milling grains creates a lot of dust. The dust is flammable and a spark can cause it to explode. You should mill outside, if possible, or in a well-ventilated space and clean up all the dust afterward.

Sounds perfect, doesn't it? Unfortunately, the electric motor base for the Family Grain Mill is not available at this time. It was made in Germany. The company went out of business and was bought by another. The distributor insists that the new company is currently integrating the electric motor base into their product line and it will be available sometime in 2011. As of December 2010 there is no concrete time when this product will be available, if at all. That throws a wrench in the works. Fortunately, the manual parts of the Family Grain Mill can be attached to other electric motor bases. This requires an adaptor and extra costs.

The Family Grain Mill is imported into the United States solely by Cris Enterprises (www.grainmill.com). However, it is carried by many distributors, all of which are listed on the Cris Enterprises website. Pleasant Hill Grains (www.pleasanthillgrains.com) offers very good prices and you can mix and match the basic unit with many attachments. You may read about it in detail at http://www.pleasanthillgrain.com/family_grain_mills.aspx.

I recommend the Family Grain Mill despite the electric motor issue. Here are your options:

☑ If, at the time you are preparing to order the Family Grain Mill, the matching electric motor base is available again, purchase the mill in both its manual and the electric motor base immediately. The entire unit should cost about $320. (The electric motor base is currently priced at $180. It may not be that price once it becomes available again.) If you want to add attachments such as the flaker or meat grinder, check out the prices and order accordingly.

TIP:
If you are going to use a flaker to make oatmeal, you will need to order soft white wheat seeds as the harder varieties will not flatten but just crack.

☑ You could, of course, order the manual parts of the Family Grain Mill and cross your fingers that the electric motor base becomes available again soon. This may not be the best idea due to the uncertain world in which we live, as well as being dependant on the vagaries of the decisions of a Germany company at some unknown point in the future. However, if you don't mind grinding your grains manually in either FEND or OTG, then by all means, purchase the manual parts of the Family Grain Mill. The basic manual mill costs $140. The flaker costs an additional $140. The hand plate for mounting the mill on a surface is included in the base price.

☑ You can get a different motor base for the Family Grain Mill. Pleasant Hill Grains carried adaptors that allow the Family Grain Mill to be hooked up to Bosch, KitchenAid, Viking, or Electrox mixers. If you already own one of these mixers, the decision will be easy. If you do not, you will need to purchase another entire appliance system just to get the electric motor base. The Bosch Universal System, for instance, offers a wide range of food processing abilities.

It can knead bread dough and has a flaker attachment. It does not, however, mill grain. You can read about it in detail at http://www.pleasanthillgrain. com/Bosch_Universal_Plus_Mixer_MUM6N10UC.aspx.   The basic Bosch Universal Mixer costs $400, and the price increases depending on the features you want. If you feel you could use the food processing features, then it makes a certain amount of sense to consider the Family Grain Mill ($140) as just another attachment to your food processor. You will also need an adaptor in order to marry the two items, at a cost of $50.

And finally, if you don't like any of these options (and I don't blame you) you can review the information about the various types of grain mills and refer to the Pleasant Hill Grains website. Check out their very nice range of all types of manual and electric grain mills and purchase them accordingly. You may wish to order another brand of electric grain mill entirely, dispensing with Bosch mixers and adaptors, and purchase the Family Grain Mill (or another) for manual grinding. The staff at Pleasant Hill Grains is more than willing to help you navigate through the various options and costs, since it can all get quite daunting.

Yeast

Most of us reading this guide are city dwellers. If we want yeast, we go to the store and purchase instant rapid-rising yeast in small foil packages or jars. We most likely have never stopped to consider what yeast is, how it works, or how people one thousand years ago managed to bake bread without a handy foil packet or glass jar of instant yeast on hand.

What is yeast? Yeast is actually a single-celled micro-organism classified in the kingdom *Fungi*. (Bet you're glad you know that now!) It converts fermentable sugars in the dough into carbon dioxide, causing the dough to expand, or rise, as the gas forms little pockets. When the dough is baked, the yeast dies and the air pockets are left, giving bread its texture.

There are dry yeasts (used in bread machines) and wet yeasts (used in sourdough bread.) The yeast we buy in the supermarket in little packets (about 2-1/2 ounces each) or in jars has been dried, and is revitalized when it is moistened in the bread-making process.

Storing dried yeast in the freezer in a sealed container will extend its life to about one year. Some say that it can last up to three years, but I wouldn't depend on that. You can buy yeast in a larger jar as opposed to the little packets which contain about 2-1/2 teaspoons.

However, once the jar is opened, the yeast will last for only two weeks at room temperature, six weeks in the refrigerator and six months in the freezer. So, if you wish to purchase dried yeast for your food stockpile, then it might be wiser to buy a lot of little packets, seal the packets inside a vacuum package for extra protection, and then store them in the refrigerator (at least while you have electricity).

TIP:
There is a yeast called Saf-Yeast that comes in 16 oz. foil sacks. It is not a rapid-rise yeast, so the bread will take a little longer to rise. The recommended shelf life is one year, but some say that it is much longer. Repackaging it in smaller lots with a Seal-A-Meal and freezing them might indeed get longer shelf-life results. I don't know how long it lasts because I haven't had my stock long enough yet to find out when it officially stops working. I would recommend this product over buying packets or jars though. You can, of course, get it on Amazon.

But how did your great-grandmother bake bread if she couldn't go to the store or order from Amazon? (Indeed, how did anyone buy anything before Amazon?) Surprise! You can make your own yeast from flour and water. I leave you to the Internet or a good bread-making book, but it is easy. Once you have a source of yeast, you save some of it and use it in the next bread-making session, and so on.

So, go ahead and buy some yeast, but if it runs out or no longer works, you do not need to despair. Life will still be worth living even in a world without little foil packets of yeast.

Wheat Flours and Wheat Seeds

Most commercial flours have been bleached to make them snowy white, or enriched (that is, the nutrients have been added back in that were lost in the processing). Whole wheat flours are just that—the entire berry has been ground up so it contains the bran and the wheat germ (which is where the nutrition is).

Wheat flour purchased from the supermarket in paper sacks and properly repackaged and sealed with a Seal-A-Meal will last between one and two years.

What To Do If You Want to Buy Whole Wheat Seeds And Grind Your Own Wheat

The best part about buying wheat in bulk is that wheat berries will last indefinitely if properly stored in sealed containers. Whole wheat can last 25 to 30 years or more, but ground flour lasts only about two years.

You should know these terms if you are going to buy and mill whole wheat berries:

☑ Individual <u>whole wheat grains</u> that have not been cooked, mashed, or otherwise changed. They are often called "<u>whole wheat berries</u>".

☑ <u>Cracked wheat</u> is whole uncooked or processed berries that have been cut into coarse pieces. It cooks faster than do whole berries.

☑ <u>Bran</u> is the outer layer of the grain and contains proteins and carbohydrates. Processed flour discards all this. You can add it to your diet by mixing it into other foods.

☑ <u>Wheat</u> germ is the embryo of the wheat seed. It is also removed in processing. It comes either raw or roasted in oil. Since it can go rancid, you should purchase it in vacuum-sealed jars.

☑ <u>Farina</u> has been coarsely ground from the entire kernel or with the bran removed.

☑ There are many kinds of cereal grains besides wheat, including amaranth, quinoa, barley, buckwheat, corn, millet, oats, rice, and rye, which can be used in cooking and baking.

Buying whole wheat berries can get a bit tricky. Here are some things you need to know before you start searching for and buying bulk wheat berries:

☑ Wheat types and availability vary widely according to the part of the country and the season. Unlike at the supermarket, at the local level you can't just buy it whenever you want. Ultimately what is available, where and when, is up to Mother Nature, and you will have to plan according to her schedule.

☑ Hard red wheat (good for making bread) is mostly grown west of the Mississippi in the winter. Soft red wheat is mostly grown east of the Mississippi River in the winter. Most co-ops and seed dealers are going to carry the wheat that is grown around them in the season in which it is going to be planted. Therefore, wheat seeds which are plentiful in November are pitifully scarce in January, and not all types of wheat seeds are going to be available in your geographic area. However, no matter where you live, you can get any kind of wheat through the Internet and have it shipped, usually in 40 to 50 lb. pails. There is the matter of shipping, which can get a bit expensive if you live in Rhode Island and are ordering from Nebraska.

☑ Different wheat seeds produce different kinds of bread. Hard red wheat is higher in protein and produces a robust-textured bread, whereas hard white wheat produces a lighter colored, more spongy loaf. Soft wheat seeds are better for rolls and other breads. A good bread-making-by-hand book, or a search on the Internet, will explain the various types of wheat and what they are good for in more detail.

☑ Wheat seeds that have been processed as forage for animals or for commercial planting are treated with various pesticides, hormones, etc. If the seed has been treated, it will usually be dyed a color (such as red or blue) to show that it is not meant for human consumption. Wheat seeds in their natural form are beige. The description "hard red wheat berries" is not a color description, but a description of the variety of wheat berry.

☑ You can check on Amazon for wheat seeds or berries. Each dealer claims they are the best, but it might be wise to call the dealer before ordering. The seeds must be <u>untreated</u> and preferably <u>non-hybrid</u>. That way, if you decide to plant them instead of grind them, you can use the seeds from last year's crop to grow the next. Hybrid seeds won't reproduce the next year nearly as well, or at all. Amazon carries small bags (5 lb, 10 lb, etc.) which, if you are trying to store up hundreds of pounds of grain, are a bad way to go about it. They do sell (at this time) a 45 lb. bag of hard red wheat in a plastic sack, but it will not only have to be shipped, it will also have to be repackaged in an air-tight pail with some kind of oxygen depletion method to keep down bugs for long-term storage.

☑ Depending on where you live, you will probably have to work the phones and Internet to see if you can find a local co-op or farmers seed store in the area. Remember, you cannot use animal or commercial seeds for human consumption, so be sure you know what you are buying. Developing a relationship with a local farmer(s) would be ideal, especially for an OTG world situation.

☑ You can also order wheat seeds from the Internet. The best place I have found for 45 lb. buckets of wheat is Pleasant Hill Grain, www.pleasanthillgrain. com. The price of wheat obviously goes up and down, and shipping will be a major factor. On the other hand, the grain is already sealed into a plastic bucket and no more processing is required. If you want to search around, put in "hard red wheat seeds" or "hard red wheat berries" into a search engine and do your own research. The closer your source, the less the shipping, which is not inconsiderable.

TIP:
One cup of wheat berries makes about 1-1/2 cups of flour (depending on the fineness). Thus one 45 lb. pail of wheat seeds will give you about 70 cups of flour.

I really recommend that you call the dealer before ordering this important item to make sure you are on the right track. This whole issue can be very confusing, especially when ordering from the Internet where they use words that are more market-oriented (such as "organic", which doesn't actually tell you all that much). I have universally found that the folks on the other end of the phone line at these places are cheerful, well-informed, and actually like to talk with you. It's a fun experience.

Gardening

Finally, another way to supplement your food supply from outside sources, or replace it if the crisis goes on long enough, is growing your own food. You should read the gardening chapter for the items you need to grow a garden for the long haul.

Now you will have to decide on your strategy for purchasing food and whether you want to pursue any of the alternatives to commercially-produced food.

Using the Forms

☑ Use Worksheet #2: **Bulk Food Calculation Worksheet** (Appendix A) to determine how much food your family will need in one year, then divide or multiply as necessary.

☑ Set up a **Shopping List** (Appendix B) for each type of food you will be buying: food from the supermarket, food in bulk from a farmers market or direct buy store, etc. Label each sheet accordingly, and follow the instructions that are with the form.

☑ You will probably want to set up a separate **Shopping list** for food making equipment as that will probably come mostly from the Internet as opposed to a supermarket. If you do not own an electric bread maker, automatic rice cooker, or crock pot, you should add them to your equipment list. As long as there is electricity, these items will make cooking and baking much easier. All three are inexpensive and can be found in any department store or on the Internet.

☑ As you purchase food items, cross them off your **Shopping List** and enter them on a corresponding **Inventory Form** (Appendix C). Label it appropriately. You should try to update the **Inventory Form** after every shopping trip, otherwise you will shortly lose track of what you have and what you need, especially if you have marked and hidden it.

SECTION 2.1: FOOD 3-5-7 TRACK

Goal: To be able to eat for three-to-seven days during a short-term emergency.

In 3-5-7 you have to eat up what you have in the refrigerator before it spoils, so the first day or two isn't a problem. Food that is kept in a freezer will keep for a couple of days without power if you avoid opening the door. You can plug the freezer into a generator (if you have one) to keep the food from spoiling. If all else fails (and you have a gas stove or Crisis Cooker, as well as a pressure canner), you could always just can everything in the freezer to keep from losing it.

A small stock of food stored for a short emergency will allow most of us to get through a few more days after the refrigerator is empty. Putting in a store of canned goods and easy-to-prepare dried packaged foods (macaroni-and-cheese-type items) will tide you over until the crisis passes.

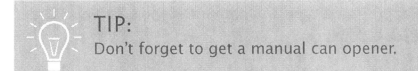

TIP:
Don't forget to get a manual can opener.

However, if there are those in your household who may need special food or nutrition (such as infants, pregnant women, elderly or persons who are sick), you should take some care in getting in a basic stock of whatever they need.

That's it! Just stock several day's worth of additional basic food and you're done!!

SECTION 2.2: FOOD FEND TRACK

Goal: To be able to offset rising food costs in tight economic conditions, or to store food that may become sporadically unavailable, rationed, or completely unavailable for long periods of time.

Adopting a Food Shopping Strategy for the FEND Track

First, decide the length of time and the number of people for which you want to prepare.

Second, research the possibility of purchasing freeze-dried food from the Internet.

<ins>If you find you can pursue the freeze-dried core food option</ins>:

Step 1:

Decide which dealer has the appropriate type and amount of food for you. Order it. When it arrives, store and/or hide it.

Step 2:

Use the **FOOD SHOPPING LIST** to list any additional foods you wish to buy at the supermarket to supplement your core food stock.

Step 3:

Use the **BULK FOOD SHOPPING LIST** to list any purchases of bulk food items such as wheat seeds, salt, sprouts, etc. that you wish to purchase from the Internet or local farmers market.

Step 4:

Use the **FOOD APPLIANCE SHOPPING LIST** to list any equipment you will need if you are going to undertake alternatives to commercially produced food. For instance, if you wish to start sprouting, put a sprouter, or sprouters, on your list. If you wish be able to mill your own bread flour, put a grain mill on your list. If you are concerned about baking in a non-electric world, put a solar oven on your Appliance List. Order them, and then check them off when the items arrive.

Those of you who cannot afford to buy a year's worth of freeze-dried food (including myself) should follow these steps:

Step 1:

Use the **FOOD SHOPPING LIST** to begin compiling the food you wish to purchase from the supermarket.

 TIP:
You may want to take a few moments on your next trip to the supermarket to browse through the aisles, giving some creative thought to the ways you can mix and match foods that will be nutritious, filling, and inexpensive. This is also the moment—before you begin shopping—to locate and visit a farmers market or bulk store, and investigate the types and sizes of foods they carry to maximize your purchasing power.

Remember that you will have to purchase a Seal-A-Meal and plastic rolls to store the food that comes in plastic sacks, paper sacks, or boxes.

 TIP:
It is best to mark the cans with the date of purchase after each shopping trip. Shopping for multiple items of food can quickly get out of hand from an organizational point of view. Trying to catch up later can be daunting—even impossible. After you have sealed the necessary food products, label the sealed packages with the name of the food stuff and date of purchase. It is also best to seal the food after each purchase, as this job can quickly snowball into a much-delayed, weekend-long mess. I know—been there, done that. I didn't like it.

Step 2:

Use the **BULK FOOD CALCULATION WORKSHEET** to determine how much food you are likely to need for the number of people and length of time you have chosen. This number can serve not only as a goal, but as a benchmark for your progress.

Step 3:

Use the **BULK FOOD SHOPPING LIST** to list any purchases of bulk food items such as wheat, salt, sprouts, etc. that you wish to purchase from the Internet or local farmers market.

Step 4:

Use the **FOOD APPLIANCE SHOPPING LIST** to list any equipment you will need if you are going to undertake alternatives to commercial food purchases. For instance, if you wish to start sprouting, put a sprouter or sprouters, on your list. If you wish to be able to mill your own bread flour, put a grain mill on your list. If you are concerned about baking in a non-electric world, put a solar oven on your Appliance List. Order them and then check them off when the items arrive.

Step 5:

Decide what, if any, freeze-dried foods you wish to buy to supplement your supermarket food. Use the **BULK FOOD SHOPPING LIST** to keep track of the vendor and the items you wish to buy as they fit into your budget.

A General List of Recommended Food Items
To Purchase From the Supermarket

Dried Foods

- ☑ Noodles and pastas of all types, including (if you can stand it) macaroni and cheese dinners, and any other inexpensive dinner mixes such as Hamburger Helper or other brand names. Get the tuna dinners because you may have little or no meat on hand, and you can stock cans of tuna. Ramen noodles are also good and very inexpensive.
- ☑ Beans of all types, including soy, lentil, and mung beans (for sprouting or cooking)
- ☑ White rice
- ☑ Dried onions, soups, potatoes, etc.
- ☑ Pre-packaged bean mixes and any dried soup mixes
- ☑ Individual packets of sauces with which to make rice and noodle dinners
- ☑ Beef jerky
- ☑ Tapioca

When purchasing dried foods, it would be wise to check the local farmers markets or markets that cater to the restaurant trade. They will carry larger and more economical units of all these things.

Canned Goods

- ☑ Vegetables, potatoes, soups, and fruits
- ☑ Cans of tomato sauce and/or diced tomatoes
- ☑ Chicken and beef broths
- ☑ Canned meats and tuna fish
- ☑ Hashes, chilis, stews, spaghettis, etc.

Breakfast Foods

- ☑ Basic cereals or granolas
- ☑ Oatmeal, Cream of Wheat, etc.

Grains and Bread-Making Supplies

- ☑ Flour (You should consider investing at least part of your budget in the actual seeds, which last a lot longer, if possible.)
- ☑ Yeast
- ☑ Popcorn (Surprisingly nutritious, popcorn keeps for a long time and it can be popped in a solar oven, if necessary.)
- ☑ Corn meal

Cooking Supplies

- ☑ Vegetable oils
- ☑ Olive oils (nutritious, can be used to cook with, and contains fats that are good for you)
- ☑ Baking soda and baking powder

Herbs, Spices, Accents, Sweeteners

- ☑ Salt and pepper
- ☑ Garlic
- ☑ Vinegar

☑ Bouillon cubes (chicken and beef)

☑ Unusual flavorings for soups, such as wonton soup mix, etc.

☑ Any spices and herbs of preference

☑ Honey

Drinks

☑ Tea bags or loose tea, including any herbal tea bags you like to drink

☑ Coffee (Include a stove-top percolator to make it in and extra filters for the coffee maker. If you can find it, get coffee beans in bulk—they'll store longer.)

☑ Dried juice drinks

☑ Powdered milk

Treats

☑ Peanut butter and jelly

☑ Granola

☑ Dried fruits and nuts

☑ Breakfast bars

☑ Cookies, crackers

Special Items

☑ Protein drink mixes (Add water or milk and some kind of flavoring to make it like a milk shake—tasty and good for you.)

☑ Cans of chocolate milk mix

☑ Fresh potatoes (If for planting, keep them refrigerated until you wish them to sprout eyes.)

This list is meant to be a general guide. Everyone's food tastes are different, and the stores at which you shop offer different types and brands of food. Your final list will be particular to you and your family.

SECTION 2.3: FOOD OTG TRACK

Goal: To be able to eat independently from your own food sources.

The OTG track for food is FEND on steroids. If the crisis is going to last for an undetermined amount of time, once you have eaten up you entire stock of food, you will need to:

- ☑ Grow a garden and can or dehydrate the resulting crop
- ☑ Forage for food in wooded and rural areas
- ☑ Hunt or fish
- ☑ Raise animals for eggs, milk and meat
- ☑ Barter or trade for food supplies for baking, sprouting, etc.

If a disaster of this scope does happen, you will have to develop alternative forms of food supplies. There are several strategies you can pursue now:

- ☑ You should start now learning how to garden and acquiring the equipment.

- ☑ You should try to form relationships with food growers in rural areas with whom you may be able to barter or trade for basic supplies in OTG.

- ☑ If you prepared for the FEND track with an eye to the OTG track, you should start learning how to can, sprout, dehydrate, and mill your own food.

Hopefully, in an OTG situation, local communities will begin to re-organize around survival concerns (such as getting food) before you run out of your store-bought food stocks. If you can't find one to join, start one yourself.

Foraging for food, and hunting or fishing are outside of the scope of this guide. Matthew Stein's book, *When Technology Fails*, has excellent information about these matters, and there are many other resources available for learning these techniques.

MEDICAL/DENTAL

An ounce of prevention is worth a ton of cure.

~Adapted Proverb ~

Chapter

3

The New Zealand earthquake of September 4, 2010 is an excellent example of the need to be prepared medically for at least a 3-5-7 event. In the Christchurch, New Zealand earthquake, emergency personnel and facilities were overwhelmed with 9-1-1 calls. The condition of the roads and bridges made getting to injured, or transporting the injured to the hospital, difficult or even impossible in the first critical hours. The hospitals were damaged and running in emergency mode. The seriously injured did get medical help, although it was probably delayed. Those without life-threatening injuries were referred by the hospitals to 24-hour clinics.

On February 22, 2011, Christchurch suffered another earthquake, which was much more damaging to life and property than the September 2010 event. Most residents of Christchurch were probably just getting back to normal when their whole world fell apart once again, this time much more thoroughly and devastatingly. That earthquake plunged them from a short-term 3-5-7 event into a FEND event.

What would happen if an earthquake such as the February 22, 2011 one in Christchurch struck San Francisco or Los Angeles? What if the hospitals were badly damaged, and medical personnel scattered and isolated? What if hundreds of thousands of injured people completely overwhelmed the health care system? What would happen to the people in the hospitals at the time of the catastrophe? What if the damage was so bad that the quality of medical care we have become used to was not be available for many months to come?

GENERAL INFORMATION

The first rule is: If you are uninjured in an event, the best thing to do is to <u>stay</u> uninjured. It may sound too simple, but in any emergency—especially in OTG—BE CAREFUL! Clearly you must do anything necessary to get yourself out of a life-threatening situation, but once the immediate life-threatening event is over:

☑ Do not operate dangerous machinery (such as chains saws) or use tools (axes, etc.) without help or training if you are inexperienced in their use.

☑ Be extra careful when handling broken glass or clearing debris.

☑ Avoid overstressing yourself physically if you were not an active person before the event, or have health issues. When tackling heavy or unfamiliar labor, pace yourself and take breaks. Assess the task and, if it is past your current abilities, don't do it or get help before tackling it. Nothing is going to get done if you collapse or hurt yourself badly. You might think if you lift weights or run regularly that you are fit, but that is not the same thing as doing some of the unfamiliar and exhausting chores you might be faced with now.

☑ Be careful when using knives, scissors, or ordinary household tools. A bad cut that needs stitches or gets infected can rapidly spiral out of control and become a serious medical issue.

☑ Watch where you are putting your feet on stairs, ladders, or stools. Do not climb around on dangerous, unstable surfaces unless it is absolutely necessary.

☑ Watch yourself when cooking or when you are around open flames.

Be patient and cautious, and recognize that you have limits. In FEND or OTG, your body will need to adapt to a new physical regimen. You can't bully your body into endurance.

You should have at least one good book on basic first aid. The Red Cross publishes a fine first aid book called The *American Red Cross First Aid & Safety Handbook*. You can get it on Amazon. Read the first aid book BEFORE you need it. Don't wait until someone is bleeding badly to start thumbing madly through the table of contents looking for the critical topic. You don't have to memorize it, but you should know what is in it and be able to find the critical information quickly.

Even better, if you can find a first-aid class in your area, take it. A CPR class from the local Red Cross or hospital would also be good to pursue.

Shopping Tips for Medical and Dental Supplies

It is not commonly appreciated, but pharmacies are amazing places in which to browse. Take some time and walk up and down every aisle, poke around, and look at everything. You can find the most amazing things at competitive prices. Here are a few shopping tips:

☑ Look for generic items that are identical to name brands but are half the cost. Why buy Thera-Flu for twice as much as a the drug store's brand when, what you are paying for is research and development costs, the threat of lawsuits, fancy TV commercials, and pretty boxes?   However, generics cost less not only because they don't have the development and marketing costs like the brand names do, but also because sometimes they provide less product. Most of the time you are still ahead cost-wise, but it is worth comparing the amounts in a brand name and a generic item before buying

TIP:
For cuts and scrapes, antibiotic creams and Band-Aids or bandages get used up amazingly quickly. Antibiotic creams are magic in a tube. An antibiotic cream not only protects the wound against infection, but helps it heal remarkably quickly. Buy lots of both items.

☑ Watch for sales—especially 2-for-1 sales. If the item is on your **shopping list**, you just doubled your purchasing power.

TIP:
Make sure you get plenty of large Band-Aids. Most of us have had the experience of needing a Band-Aid only to find that all that is left in the box is a Band-Aid the size of a fingernail. The larger ones are generally more useful and so are quickly used up.

☑ The box sizes for ointments, creams, and bottles of over-the-counter medicines can be misleading (to put it nicely). You open a four-inch long by one-inch square box and out falls a tiny little one-inch tube or a bottle the size of a thimble with two drops of the item in it.

That little dab cost $10? A big fat box may contain only six tablets of the product. Check the front of the box before buying to see what is actually in there. Band-aid boxes are especially misleading. There are not nearly as many Band-Aids in the box as it appears. The amount of Band-Aids in most boxes can be flattened down to about ½ inch of actual material. This is called "marketing" and technically it's not actual deception . . . but . . .

TIP:
You will want to check out the amount of the actual items in the boxes at the time you are adding it to your "home clinic." You do not want to open the box in an emergency and find you only have a tiny amount of something important.

☑ Keep your **Medical and Dental Shopping Lists** with you so you can take advantage of spot sales. You can save a lot of money this way if you have a stretch of time in which to do your shopping. If budget is an issue, get the basic items you feel you must have first, and then cruise the drug store about once a week, looking for inexpensive ways to increase your stock.

TIP:
Some items, such as Sudafed (which contains pseudoephedrine), are kept behind the counter. When I asked why Sudafed was being guarded by the pharmacist, I was told that pseudoephedrine is used in the manufacturing of illegal drugs. You have to ask for the Sudafed specifically (and other products with pseudoephedrine in them) and sign for it. Therefore, it might not be wise to ask for six boxes of Sudafed at one time. You don't want a federal SWAT team arriving the next day and kicking down your door, looking for your "drug factory". This falls under the category of "staying under the radar" when prepping.

A Word on Pain Relievers

There are so many different types of pain relievers on the market today that it is very confusing. The matter is complicated by the interchangeable use of trade names (Advil, Tylenol, Motrin, etc.) and their common name equivalents (ibuprofen, aspirin, naproxen, acetaminophen, etc.). Here is a quick rundown on the various types, their properties, and common names. It will be useful, especially if you are buying generics.

Aspirin

Brand names: Bayer, Bufferin

Aspirin is an anti-inflammatory which means it is good for headaches, minor aches and pain, and reducing inflammation in cases of arthritis, sprains, sunburns, etc. However, it is hard on the upper digestive tract and can cause upset stomach, heartburn, and dyspepsia. It is an anti-coagulant, so it is bad for hemophiliacs (but helpful in treating heart disease for the same reason). Some say that taking an aspirin a day will help prevent heart disease. It is not always safe for children.

Ibuprofen

Brand names: Motrin, Advil

Ibuprofen is also an anti-inflammatory, but it irritates the esophagus and stomach lining less than aspirin or naproxen. People with ulcers or acid reflux disease therefore find it useful.

Naproxen

Brand name: Aleve

Aleve is an anti-inflammatory. It is useful for headaches, arthritis, sunburns, and other inflammation-based pain. It seems to have an edge over the others and many women suffering from menstrual cramps find naproxen better for reducing cramps. It also lasts longer (8-to-12 hours instead of 4-to-8 hours for the others).

Acetaminophen (paracetamol)

Brand names: Tylenol

Tylenol lowers fevers and sooth headaches, but it is not an anti-inflammatory, so it won't do much for sprains or arthritis. However, it does have a milder effect on the upper digestive tract than the other pain relievers and is less irritating to the lining of the stomach. It is also safe for hemophiliacs and children. However, acetaminophen is one of the most overdosed drugs in the world. Many people overdose accidentally when they combine it with other common medicines such as cold and flu medications that also contain acetaminophen. An overdose can cause kidney and liver failure. Activated charcoal, if taken immediately after the overdose, may help prevent the body from absorbing some of the drug, but it is critical to seek immediate medical attention as activated charcoal will not be sufficient to reverse the damage. Be careful with this drug, especially if it is a FEND or OTG situation.

How To Store Your Medical and Dental Supplies

Select a closet or storage site in your home for your home clinic. If you have small children, you may want to keep anything they can drink or swallow away from their busy little hands by putting them in plastic boxes which seal tightly (and even tape them shut), and placing them on the highest shelf or in a location that makes it harder to access. You should issue firm instructions NOT TO TOUCH. Keep things like Band-Aids, bandages, splints, gloves, masks, heating pads, and similar items on the lower shelves.

You should always keep your first-aid kit, burn kit, and any supplies that may be needed immediately in a crisis, where you can reach them quickly. If there is an emergency, you don't want to be yanking out plastic bins and rummaging through them, throwing items over your shoulder in a panic looking for the antiseptics, bandages, and butterfly closures while someone is bleeding badly.

If you don't have much storage space, you should condense the items as follows:

1. For tablets, take the items out of the boxes. Cut up the box, but keep BOTH the face of the package, and the drug and dosage information on the back. Flatten the cut-up box and tuck everything into a sandwich bag. When you seal it, press all the air out of it.

2. Use a different sandwich bag for every different <u>brand name</u> (even of the same type of product) so the pills don't get mixed together. You will not be able to tell which instructions go with the unidentified blue pills or the yellow pills after they are out of the box. You may put identical brand names of the same type of medicine into the same baggie.

3. Group related items in one large gallon baggie (all laxatives, all antihistamines, etc.) When you seal it, press all the air out of it.

TIP:
Putting Band-Aids into a baggie is especially space saving as they are packaged in boxes that are mostly air. It looks like you are getting a whole boatload of Band-Aids when it is really about 15 to 20 or so per box. When you get done emptying all the Band-Aid boxes into one bag, you tend to find you don't have nearly as much as you thought. DO NOT remove sterile gauze pads or roll bandages from their packages.

4. Do not open pill bottles, anything that is packaged in sterile containers, or anything sealed with a foil top or tamper-proof method.

Flattening boxes and grouping them together in like products will save space, but it will also give you a feeling for what you actually have. They are easier to find quickly as well.

Dipping Into Your Supplies

You shouldn't touch these supplies. Use your regular medicine cabinet as required for daily use. But if you do take something out of your home clinic, mark it off the **Inventory Sheet** and put it back on your **Shopping List**.

Using the Forms

☑ Set up one **Shopping List** each for medical and dental items (Appendix B).

☑ As you purchase the items, move them off the **Shopping List** and put them on an **Inventory Form** (Appendix C).

SECTION 3.1: MEDICAL/DENTAL 3-5-7 TRACK

Goal: To be able to deal with minor cuts and punctures, fractures, sprains, scrapes, and rashes without needing immediate outside medical care.

This assumes that, in the event of a serious accident, injury, or illness, professional medical care can be accessed, although there might be a delay.

Basic First-Aid Kits

Everyone should have a good first-aid kit in both their homes and their cars. A smaller one should be stowed in one or more of your Go-Bags. For the 3-5-7 track, a first-aid kit from the store or the Internet, supplemented by a few items, is perfectly fine.

Don't get too excited by kits that shout they have "299 pieces!!" It is not the number of items, but the range of items that is important. When examining one of these kits, I found it contained two (2) aspirins and two (2) safety pins, which counted as four (4) "pieces". That same kit counted the bag it came in as another "piece"! You get the idea.

When evaluating a first-aid kit, look for one that has as much of the following as possible:

- ☑ Band-Aids of various sizes
- ☑ Sterile gauze dressings of various sizes
- ☑ Several butterfly wound closures
- ☑ Sealed antiseptic towelettes or alcohol pads for cleaning wounds
- ☑ Roll bandages (gauze or fabric)
- ☑ A roll of adhesive tape
- ☑ Scissors
- ☑ Burn relief (gels, creams, etc.)
- ☑ A thermometer
- ☑ Tweezers
- ☑ Antibacterial ointment
- ☑ Pain relief (aspirin, ibuprofen, etc.)
- ☑ A cold pack

☑ An emergency blanket

☑ Eye wash

☑ Finger splints

☑ Stabilizers for wrist, elbow, ankle, and knee

☑ Arm sling

☑ Burn kit or burn dressings and gel

☑ A first-aid guide

None of the basic kits will have all these items or, for that matter, any one item in great quantity—not even the "299 pieces!!" kit. Look at the range of items in the kit carefully and, if you think you might need more of any item or want to add anything listed above, supplement it from the store.

TIP:

If any member of your family has a serious medical condition such as diabetes, a chronic heart condition, asthma, etc. which requires prescription drugs, you should strive to keep them refilled in a proactive manner. Don't let the prescription get below a week's supply if possible. Pharmacies work on the "Just in Time" (JIT) inventory principle. When the pharmacist fills a prescription, the computer puts in an order for re-supply, which arrives the next day. If that supply line is interrupted or broken, the situation could quickly become very perilous for you or your loved one. If you suspect this might be the case, follow the rule "First come, first serve" and make the immediate refill of the prescription your highest priority.

Buying a pre-assembled first-aid kit is quick, easy, and cheap—about $15 to $25—considering you usually get scissors, tweezers, a pair of sterile gloves, etc. Individual purchases of all the items will add up to much more than the cost of the basic kit. First-aid kits are widely available in every pharmacy, department store, and on the Internet. Enter "first-aid kits" in a search engine on the Internet and you will get many different sites with much the same items at similar prices. Remember, don't judge them solely on the number of "pieces", but on what is actually in them. You might want to buy a good first-aid book as well because the ones they generally put in the kits are often little more than flimsy brochures.

TIP:
Getting a first-aid kit seems like a simple matter but, especially on the Internet, the choices can be overwhelming. There are kits for the car, children, businesses, RVs, hiking, and even for pets. Some provide kits to treat large numbers of people (50, 75, 100, and 200 persons), others are entire first-aid stations used in offices and businesses, and still others are specialized kits for industry or medical professionals (first responders and trauma units.) Generally, you may ignore most of these because you can do better by beefing up your own basic kit with items more pertinent to you. Dedicated burn kits and eye-care kits are exceptions. Either would be an excellent specialized addition to your basic first-aid supplies. You can also purchase defibrillators and CPR kits if you feel that is necessary for your situation.

Final Recommendations for the 3-5-7 Track

1. Order or buy good first-aid kits for the house, car and Go-Bags.

2. Check them out, supplement them with items that are scantily provided or which you feel are necessary for your particular family situation.

3. Purchase a good first-aid book.

That's it!! You're done with the 3-5-7 Track!

SECTION 3.2: MEDICAL/DENTAL FEND TRACK

Goal: To be able to deal with as many non-life-threatening medical situations as you can on your own, and to offset increasing costs or scarcity of commonly needed medical supplies or services over a long period of time.

Supplementing Basic First-Aid Kits for FEND

Everyone should have the basic first-aid kit described in the 3-5-7 track in their house, car and Go-Bag, but in the FEND track you will need to deepen and broaden your stock of these items.

In the pre-FEND days, you would have gone to the doctor for diagnosis and treatment for minor medical conditions, accidents, or for preventive or early diagnosis of a troubling medical circumstance. In FEND days you may find you have to take care of numerous, non-life-threatening medical issues on your own, and will have to assess if and when an injury or illness requires professional medical attention so you can bend all your attention to getting it.

If you have a family, you know that one of them always has a terrible time every spring with allergies, another could manage somehow to cut themselves on a pillow, and yet another has a temperamental digestive system that constantly makes them miserable. The elderly and sick may have ongoing medical issues such as arthritis, limited movement, or pain relief needs that require prescription drugs or ongoing medical care. Plan ahead. Stock up on the items you know your family will need over a long period of time. Even if a FEND situation never happens, it is a safe bet that, at best, the items listed below will only increase in cost over the next few years (allowing you to save money in increasingly difficult economic times) or at the worst, they may become scarce or unavailable.

Besides beefing up the minor amounts of bandages, creams, adhesive tape, etc. provided in the basic first-aid kit to reflect the potential usage for the period of time you have chosen to be prepared for, you may also want to add any or all of these items below:

- ☑ A big bottle of rubbing alcohol for disinfection

- ☑ An instant ice pack and a heating pack

- ☑ A digital thermometer

☑ Safety pins (all sizes)

☑ Scissors. If you can find an all-metal pair, that is even better because they can be sterilized if necessary.

☑ Sterile exam gloves. These are different than the latex gloves for cleaning the house. They are more supple and fit closely on the hand, allowing you to perform delicate tasks, and come in individually-packaged sterile pairs. For once, Amazon does not serve. You can get them from many places, but try www.quickmedical.com first. A box of 100 gloves costs about $30. If you cannot afford sterile exam gloves, at least purchase some nitrile exam gloves, which can be obtained from Amazon or your local drug store. They are supple and fit closely to the hand, but are not sterile.

☑ Pain killers of your choice: aspirin, acetaminophen, ibuprofen, etc. Get the biggest bottles possible in generic form.

☑ A laxative

☑ Anti-diarrhea or upset-stomach medication like Pepto-Bismol, Kaopectate, or their generic equivalent.

☑ Syrup of ipecac or a similar product to induce vomiting.

☑ Splints or protective supports for fingers, wrists, ankles, knees, etc.. They come in standard sizes, but get the adjustable size if you can.

☑ An adjustable cane (and crutches if you can afford them). Crutches are not usually sold in the drug store but can be ordered from the Internet.

☑ An arm sling

☑ Burn gel or a burn kit

☑ Antacids or heartburn medications

☑ A good supply of physician-quality face masks. You want the kind doctors wear, not the fiber nose-cup kind that are really only good for dust and the like. They are expensive ($3 to $5 each) but you should have as many as possible for each member of your family. They were all over the place during the recent big flu "epidemic." If you see them, grab them up or ask the pharmacist where they are hiding them now that the "crisis" is over.

☑ Epsom salts

☑ A hefty supply of Purell, or some similar disinfectant

☑ Pediatric electrolyte solution or similar (for restoring body water and minerals lost in diarrhea and vomiting). Gatorade also replaces electrolytes in cases of dehydration.

☑ Anti-histamines or allergy relief remedies.

☑ Itch relief cream (topical analgesic). Another good item to have a lot of in your kit. Scratching at rashes and insect bites can make an annoying situation a lot worse. Calamine lotion is another version of itch relief.

☑ Eye wash (for washing out foreign items from the eye). Be careful, this is not the same as contact lens cleaner. They look very similar and in a pinch I expect they'd work much the same. But the eye wash comes with a cup on top of it that you can use to flush out the eye. (You can also purchase an eye-care emergency kit if you wish.)

☑ Eye allergy relief. This tends to be one of those tiny little bottles the size of a flea that comes in a big box with a correspondingly big price tag. But it will help with itchy eyes where the eye wash won't.

☑ Cold and flu medicine. Read the label of the kind you want and match it up to a less expensive generic product.

☑ Sore throat lozenges or sprays

☑ Saline nasal spray

☑ Vaseline

☑ Medicated lip balm

☑ Pain relieving balms (like Hot & Icy) for muscle pains, aches, and strains. Look for a generic label as Hot & Icy is the brand name.

☑ Heating and cooling pads for sore muscles and strains.

☑ Aloe vera gel. Aloe vera is in a lot of cosmetics, lotions and over-the-counter medicines. Get the pure gel if you can find it. A medium-sized bottle can be found in most health food stores or on the Internet. You can't have too much aloe vera either. It's amazing.

☑ A vaporizer, Vicks Vaporub, or similar product.

☑ Lots of Q-tips, cotton balls and/or cosmetic squares. However, when one package of cotton swabs is a lot cheaper than another, there is a reason: there's less cotton on the tip. I spend a little extra money here and buy the good ones, as I don't like the idea of sticking a toothpick with a faint gauze layer on it in my ears or other delicate places.

☑ Insect repellant sprays

☑ Suntan lotion or creams

☑ Heating pad (with moist heat)

☑ Water bottle (hot or cold)

These things should get you through minor injuries and illnesses such as sprains, insect bites, rashes, shallow cuts, minor bouts of diarrhea or upset stomach, common headaches, mild toothache, colds and flu, or other common illnesses. The insect repellant sprays and suntan lotion may not seem like a "medical" item, but they fall nicely into the category of "an ounce of prevention is worth a ton of cure."

Add any items that are particular to your family's routine medical issues such as allergies, breathing difficulties, specific types of pain relief, supplies for any ongoing medical condition, duplicate insulin testers, and/or any medical supplies specifically required by your family.

Dental Supplies

In addition to deepening your stock of medical supplies, you should also purchase some dental supplies.

☑ Ambesol or Orajel (for minor tooth pain until you can get to the dentist)

☑ Filling repair kits. The box warns that it is meant only as a temporary fix, but it will help tide you over until you can find a dentist. Your dentist will have a fit when you finally show up and he sees what you have done to your mouth, so be ready for a stern dental lecture. Tough. I've never met a dentist who liked anything that was sold in a drug store except tooth brushes, toothpaste, and floss. They've got about 800 different reasons why it's all rubbish and the only answer is $5,000 worth of expensive custom dental treatment.

For long-term dental management, they have a point but those were the old days . . . these are the FEND days. It's your mouth and your pain. They'll survive.

☑ An electric toothbrush brush replacement (for when the current one breaks down) or extra tooth brushes

☑ Replacement electric toothbrush heads

☑ Toothpaste

☑ Mouthwash

☑ Floss or picks

☑ Any other dental item you use for dentures, etc.

Remember, especially in the area of dental care, <u>an ounce of prevention is worth a ton of cure</u>. It would be very, very wise to become obsessive about your teeth starting ten minutes ago. If it is possible, you should get them in shape now and then keep them that way. Dental pain is surreal and soul-destroying. You will not be able to function in the FEND or OTG world if you are lost in a haze of pain. You don't even want to <u>think</u> about someone pulling your teeth with pliers.

Other Resources

In FEND, you should also invest in a comprehensive health book such as, or similar to, the *Harvard Medical School Family Health Guide* (Simon & Schuster, 1999). You need a resource that explains how our bodies work and how to diagnose potential health issues. It may help you make some tough decisions about when you do need to access professional health care and when you can help yourself. If you happen to have a medical professional in your family or social network—even a veterinarian or a dental hygienist—you are truly blessed.

If you purchased Matthew Stein's, *When Technology Fails*, he also has a section on first aid, including CPR, controlling bleeding, treating injuries (including stitches), helping someone who is choking, treating shock, fractures and dislocations, sprains, bites, heat stroke, how to move injured people, and emergency childbirth.

Finally, purchase a resource on home remedies. *Prevention Magazine* has a wonderful resource called *The Doctor's Book of Home Remedies*, but there are others equally as useful.

These are your grandma's remedies and are usually a collection of common sense advice and readily available options for treating a wide variety of health issues.

It is important to understand that just ordering these books and putting them on your bookshelf is not enough. You must at least scan them, and preferably read them, before an emergency. Some of the advice in the home remedies books will be useful in your daily life now and do not require an emergency to use them.

Vitamins, Herbs and Homeopathic Medicines

Since your diet may be restricted or rationed during FEND, large bottles of daily vitamins may come in handy. But before you start buying expensive bottles of Vitamin This and Vitamin That for various perceived lacks and disorders, you may want to take a little time with a remarkable resource: *Prescription of Nutritional Healing: A Practical A-Z Reference To Drug-Free Remedies Using Vitamins, Minerals, Herbs & Food Supplements* by James and Phyllis Balch. This book should become your bible on vitamins and supplements. Hundreds of disorders and their treatment from a nutritional perspective are outlined in detail. It also includes useful discussions on vitamins, minerals, water, amino acids, antioxidants, enzymes, natural food supplements, and herbs. Amazon carries the title new or used, and it is worth every dime.

Those who prefer homeopathic, natural, or herbal preparations for preventative purposes, or for treating common ailments or injuries are probably already familiar with their local health food store or herb shop. You should stock up on items you have found useful in the past and which, in an emergency, will become very hard or impossible to get. A very good resource on natural alternatives to over-the-counter and prescription medicines is *The Herbal Drugstore* by Linda B. White and Steven Foster. It explores the treatment options for a wide variety of medical issues, listing the prescription or over-the-counter drugs and then offering natural alternatives. You can find it on Amazon.

However, there are a few natural preparations everyone should have in their FEND medicine chest:

☑ **Charcoal tablets.** They are a very effective treatment for mild food poisoning or situations where you may have taken in toxic contaminants. Basically it passes right through your body, binding toxins to it as it goes. It can also be used in powder form to draw out toxins through the skin. Ask at your local health food store because charcoal tablets or capsules come in many different names and dosages, and they can guide you through the several shelves of confusing alternatives available. You can also find it at Amazon.

☑ **Dirt.** Or, more specifically, a clay called kaolin. It's all over the ground—no, it IS the ground—in southeastern Georgia. It neutralizes poisons in the intestinal tract, soothes digestive afflictions, and enriches and balances the blood. Like charcoal, it passes through you body and, as it goes, it draws bacteria, viruses, toxins, and even radiation along with it. The clay adsorbs them (yes, that is the correct spelling). It can be used internally and externally. You can find kaolin at Amazon. Don't forget that you will need empty gelatin capsules to take it internally.

 TIP:
Bentonite clay is an option to kaolin. You can usually find it in pre-packaged or bulk form at an herbal store or from the Internet.

When I learned about the ability of clay to draw out toxins, I remembered that, when I was a young child, my grandmother, my brother, and me were out in the woods near my grandparent's farm, picking raspberries. As my brother rummaged in the bushes, he stirred up a wasp's nest. The wasps surged out and surrounded us in an angry cloud. We were both stung many times. It was a terrifying experience and I still pathologically hate bees of any kind today. My grandmother covered the bites with clay to draw out the toxins. We looked like we had both fallen into a mud hole, but it worked!!

☑ **Potassium Iodide.** Finally, if you are concerned about the possibility of being exposed to nuclear radiation (as happened in the Chernobyl nuclear disaster in Russia in 1986), you should look into acquiring some potassium iodide tablets. Potassium iodine is NOT regular iodine. This drug is approved by the FDA and protects the thyroid gland from absorbing radioactive iodine from accidents or fission emergencies. If you are interested in getting potassium iodide, you should enter "potassium iodide" in Wikipedia and read about it before buying. The product can be obtained on the Internet, including at: http://www.nukepills.com. They are not expensive.

An excellent resource for persons who wish to learn to prepare their own home herbal remedies is *Herbal Preparations and Natural Therapies*: *Creating and Using a Home Herbal Medicine Chest* by Debra St. Claire. This kit contains a laboratory reference manual that teaches you how to prepare infusions, decoctions, lozenges, tinctures, fluid extracts for liniments, salves, ointments, creams, compresses, and powders and explains how to use them. The course contains three DVDs with four hours of video instruction. You will need some basic supplies such as jars, pans, mixing bowls, gelatin capsules, and various kitchen items, as well as a basic stock of oils, lanolin, and herbs. The course costs $150 plus shipping. You may read about it and order it at http://www.makeherbalmedicines.com.

In conjunction with the herbal course, you can also purchase a beginning stock of herb seeds in the form of the Survival Herb Bank: Herbal Remedies Crisis Garden so you can grow your own herbs for medicines. It contains many common herb seeds, including catnip, arnica, feverfew, boneset, valerian, black cohosh, Echinacea, Florence fennel, evening primrose, calendula, chicory, comfrey, chamomile, lavender, cayenne, yarrow, rosemary, lemon balm, hyssop, and marshmallow. The herb bank costs about $100 plus shipping. You may read about it and order it at http://www.survivalherbbank.com/. You also get a free companion e-book called *How To Grow Your Own Herbs for Survival Remedies*.

Those who are really committed to learning how to prepare herbal remedies can also enroll in one of many online colleges which offer certificates in natural health, holistic nutrition, and herbalism. This approach requires a minimum commitment of several years. However, it is worth considering since Obamacare will eventually discourage many people from seeking health care for relatively minor medical issues because of the waiting period and bureaucratic issues. There may be a real niche in the next few years for qualified holistic practitioners to fill the rationing and bureaucracy gap. However, the current indications are that the government isn't going to like folks helping themselves and escaping from under their thumb. It is not completely impossible that they will ban such education and/or homeopathic, herbal, and natural remedies under the guise of "consumer protection" in the future.

Final Recommendations for the FEND Track

1. Purchase good first-aid kits for the house, the car, and your Go-Bags.

2. Examine the first-aid kits. Whatever they put in there, decide how you want to supplement the basic stock.

3. Write it all down on the **Shopping List**.

4. Start shopping. If you are on a tight budget, start with the absolute essentials at a minimal level, then increase the number and extent of the items as budget permits. Trawl through the medical sections of department stores and drug stores looking for sales and generic items.

5. As you acquire items, write them on the **Inventory Form** and reduce or erase them from your **Shopping List**.

6. Remove them from their boxes and group them if you need to save space, and put them on a high secure shelf or in a closet (preferably one you can lock). Keep the **Inventory Form** near your home clinic.

7. Make sure that you have a comprehensive first-aid book; a volume on general health issues and the working of the human body; home remedies; and vitamins and nutrition in your library. You should read them, or at least be familiar with their contents.

8. Take classes at local hospitals or the Red Cross in your area on first-aid and CPR, as time and budget permits.

9. As a long-term goal, you may wish to learn to prepare homeopathic medicines on your own, either through home instruction or an accredited college.

SECTION 3.3:
MEDICAL/DENTAL OTG TRACK

Goal: To stay alive, in one piece and reasonably healthy, until a modicum of medical services returns to the community.

The medical OTG track is a perfect example of why most people simply can't face preparing. The idea that medical and dental care may only be sporadic or completely unavailable for an extended period of time causes them to seize up and just turn away from the whole issue.

I can appreciate the impulse, as I have it myself when it comes to this topic. Denial is a powerful human defense mechanism, which sometimes stands us in good stead. Unfortunately, we cannot afford to look away from this issue.

This level requires not only the acquisition of medical supplies, but the possible application of skills you have not previously had and, more than likely, don't really want. However, you have no choice. If there is a medical or dental professional of any kind in your family or social network—even a veterinarian or a dental hygienist—you should give thanks.

In the OTG track, medical and dental care becomes your own responsibility for an unknown amount of time. Those persons with pre-existing medical conditions, or who require drugs or medical care to support life, are in real trouble for which little or nothing can be done. Ordinary medical issues such as appendicitis, so easily handled in the non-OTG world, can become killers. In these situations, you or your loved ones are in God's hands.

In the OTG track, you may want to acquire some sterile suture needles and suture material, if you think you can actually handle stitching someone up. These can be bought on Amazon (put in "sterile sutures") for about $20 for a quantity of 12. (Amazon is amazing, isn't it?) Those of you who feel competent at providing serious medical care can order surgical instruments as well.

However, they are very pricey at $1,200 and above per instrument kit. Surgical scissors are not cheap either.

Start Reading Now: Books You Must Have

You should purchase the small library listed in the FEND track, along with these two books:

- ☑ *Where There is No Doctor: A Village Health Care Handbook* by David Werner (revised edition) (Hesperian, 2009).

- ☑ *Where There Is No Dentist* by Murray Dickson (Hesperian, 2009).

Both books are written for the community health care worker based in countries or rural settings without immediate access to modern medical systems.

Both are infinitely practical, simply written, and packed with basic information on a variety of subjects. Both may be obtained from Amazon.

Where There is No Doctor contains information on:

- ☑ Dealing with broken bones and dislocations, including making homemade casts
- ☑ Different sicknesses and ailments, and their causes
- ☑ How to examine a sick person
- ☑ Healing without medicines
- ☑ Antibiotics—what they are and how to use them
- ☑ How to measure and give medicine, including instructions for giving injections
- ☑ General first-aid (how to control bleeding, treating cuts and wounds, how to stitch up wounds, and dealing with infections and serious wounds)
- ☑ Dealing with parasites and *giardia*
- ☑ Treating common sicknesses (dehydration, diarrhea and dysentery, headaches and migraines, colds and flu, allergies, asthma, arthritis, back pain, skin, eye, and urinary problems)
- ☑ Dental issues dealing with teeth, gums, and mouth
- ☑ Pregnancy and childbirth
- ☑ Detailed information on medicines (such as antibiotics) and their dosages for common illnesses

Where There Is No Dentist covers:

- ☑ Basic information on dental care management

- ☑ Treating common problems such as cavities, abscesses, loose teeth, gum disease, and other dental, mouth, and jaw related issues

- ☑ How to remove teeth and treatment afterwards

- ☑ Cleaning your teeth.

In the absence of dental and medical care, these books will be invaluable.

REMEMBER: Information contained in this book is intended as an educational aid only. Information is not intended as medical advice for individual conditions or treatment, and is not a substitute for a medical examination, nor does it replace the need for services provided by medical professionals.

Final Recommendations for the OTG Track

There is little to add in OTG over FEND. You should:

1. Order *Where There Is No Dentist* and *Where There is No Doctor*, and read them.

2. If you are really committed or have the skills, you may wish to order sterile sutures and any medical instruments you feel you can handle.

SECURITY

*If someone has a gun and is trying to kill you,
it would be reasonable to shoot back with your
own gun*

~ The Dalai Lama, Seattle Times, May 15, 2001 ~

Chapter

4

In New Orleans, in the aftermath of Hurricane Katrina, the most dangerous two-legged animals were not the looters, but those who reveled in violence. They immediately perceived they had been handed a key to their own personal Garden of Eden. According to Douglas Brinkley in *The Great Deluge: Hurricane Katrina, New Orleans, and the Mississippi Gulf Coast*, a kind of "wilding" occurred. Criminals broke into private residences, regardless of whether the residents were home, and terrorized them for fun. They took what they wanted and the residents were lucky to keep their lives. One man was forced to hold off intruders trying to get into his kitchen window with the only weapon he had—a tire iron. He and his family couldn't even leave their home as the police—what there was left of them—had been authorized to shoot to kill. He and his family cowered inside their house for days until the situation began to stabilize. This man and his family was both brave and lucky—they survived. But imagine a similar situation for a longer period of time. Are you ready to protect your own life and the lives of your loved ones?

GENERAL INFORMATION

It certainly can't hurt to be more security-conscious in this age of home invasions and rising crime. If you do not wish to have a firearm in the house, there are a few things you can do:

☑ If it is legal in your state, purchase some type of pepper spray or a similar product. Put them on your keychain, in the car, by your bed and around the house. There may be situations where pepper spray might discourage an intruder or attacker and let you get away, but you are in a very dangerous situation if you are close enough to the intruder to be able to use it accurately. However, it should not to be discounted as a tool of last resort. Having pepper spray on your keychain or in the car, however, makes a great deal of sense and is highly recommended. A personal panic alarm for your keychain might also be useful. You can get both inexpensively at www. thehomesecuritysuperstore.com.

☑ Get a 24-hour monitored security system for your house. Strategically placed motion-sensitive flood lights and video cameras are also a good investment. However, if the electricity is out they are, of course, useless. Put that "Protected by . . ." sign prominently in front of the house and the stickers all over your windows and doors.

☑ If you can't afford a security system, video cameras, and lights, you can purchase generic stickers for your lawn, windows and doors. Even neater are inexpensive fake cameras that move and flash like they are taking pictures. You can also buy a door-alarm security bar, wireless alarms, magnetic contact alarms for windows and doors, motion detectors, and driveway alarms, all which do not work on electricity and all inexpensive. One interesting item is called the Super Door Stop Wedge Alarm. This is an electronic doorstop that alerts, warns, and stops intruders all in one. When the door is pushed back against this doorstop, it activates a 120-decibel siren and the unit wedges underneath the door, preventing further entry. It takes a 9-volt battery. Obviously, it's no good on sliding glass doors, but on any other door that opens inward it could be a life saver. It costs $8.95 on the http:// www.thehomesecuritysuperstore.com site. All of the products above are also available there.

☑ You could get a couple of really, really big mean attack dogs. But if you have children, they may be more of a concern than owning a firearm you can at least lock up.

☑ Even if you don't own a big mean dog, you can still post a big sign saying "Beware of Dog." You can also get an intriguing item called the Radar Surveillance Watch Dog. It senses motion within 20 feet and starts barking like a vicious German shepherd. As the person gets closer to it, the barking gets louder and more frequent. It can work through wood, cement, brick, metal, glass, paper, air, cardboard, curtains, and more. It may divert criminals or intruders looking for an easy target, and they'll go away to rob or hurt someone else. You can get it from www.thehomesecuritysuperstore.com for $70. Good luck with this plan, but it's better than nothing.

☑ Personal self defense classes, if you can find one in your area, are not a bad idea either.

Concerning Firearms

In the aftermath of Hurricane Katrina, we saw graphically on TV what a temporarily lawless world looked like after just a few days, and it was ugly. These conditions can occur in any of the three tracks—just for different lengths of time. In a disaster or long-term crisis situation, the police may not be able to get there in a reasonable time, if at all. If the electricity is off and communications are broken down, all the fancy electronic equipment in the world is useless.

At this time, as an American citizen, you are entitled to own a firearm to provide your own "Thin Blue Line" in a situation where your life, or the lives of your family, is in immediate and deadly peril. That is, of course, unless you live a community like Chicago or Washington, D.C. that have unconstitutionally usurped your rights to defend yourself. Recently, banning guns was dealt a blow by a court case in which that practice was ruled unconstitutional. Even so, the communities will find one thousand administrative ways to make it all but impossible for their citizens to be able to own guns (i.e., oppressive taxes or registration fees on any firearm you own, etc.). In such a situation, if the possibility arises, vote with your feet and move some place your constitutional rights are not summarily abridged by bureaucrats.

If you have a family, you have a responsibility to defend them. And understandably, if you have a family, your concerns about owning a firearm are probably intense. In fact, there is a very real danger from firearms that are not properly secured in a home (especially with children in it) that cannot be disregarded. However, gun safes with push-button mechanical or electronic keyboards are available. Such a safe can be accessed quickly with a combination known only to you and still be inaccessible to children or thieves.

If you are unfamiliar with firearms (and unless you know someone who can advise you competently about firearm safety, loading and unloading, and teach you to shoot cans unerringly off a fence on someone's farm or to punch holes in a paper target at a firing range), then you should enroll in a firearm safety course at a local firing range BEFORE you purchase a firearm. These courses are not expensive. In them you will learn how to handle a variety of guns safely, and shoot them for practice under supervision. The firearms safety instructor is a competent professional and can advise you on the best purchase for your needs and capabilities. Then practice, practice, and practice some more until you can handle the gun safely in your sleep and in the dark. You can purchase snap caps, or dummy ammunition, with which to practice loading and unloading. This way, you cannot hurt yourself or anyone else. The worst you can do is drop the gun on your toe. Some gun shops or shooting ranges also have people who, for a fee, will individually instruct you in firearm use and home-defense strategies.

Any child of responsible age should be included in the firearms safety class and taught to use the weapon safely and properly. Do you ban your children of responsible age from using a knife to cut up carrots for dinner, grabbing it hysterically from their hand, banishing them to their room without supper and with stern warnings, and then lock the knife up in a safe? No. You instruct them on the safe ways to use a knife. "Don't run with that, please." "Be more careful. You're going to cut your fingers. Here, hold it like this, okay?" "Take that away from your baby sister, please, and put it on the counter."

If you just can't deal with the idea of owning a gun, it still can't hurt to take a firearms safety class. No one will make you buy a gun afterwards if you still can't abide the idea.

LAUGH: IT'S GOOD FOR YOU. One of the gun shops I go to is in a strip mall. Four doors down is a meditation and yoga center. Every time I go there I laugh out loud at the placement of the two storefronts. The karma-heads down at the meditation and yoga center probably park their cars WAY down the parking lot or across the street—never grasping that crossing the street is about 12,000 times more dangerous than the presence of a gun shop full of competent marksmen on their doorstep. I wonder how they "om" with all that bad karma oozing out under the gun shop's door and creeping down there. They also may not realize that that is one strip mall that probably won't be robbed—at least during business hours.

Of course, the best thing of all is never having to use a firearm in a defense situation. If you hear someone downstairs, racking a pump shotgun (which makes a <u>very</u> distinctive sound) will, in the words of an instructor I once had, cause the intruder to "leave so fast they'll leave an man-shaped hole in the wall."

Gun Laws and Regulations and Self-Defense

If you are going to own a firearm, you must also learn what the gun laws and laws on self-defense are in your state, and comply with them absolutely. The state has the power to imprison you if you violate them. When purchasing a firearm, you will have to give the dealer personal information which he submits to the FBI via computer, which performs a background check on you as you wait. It may take thirty minutes but, if you don't have a criminal record, there is no reason you can be denied the purchase of the firearm.

If you eventually wish to acquire a carry permit, the process may be purposefully discouraging. Like the communities that ban guns, they make it so hard and expensive, and you have to wait so long that you don't even want to bother. In a previous county in which I lived, you had to jump through so many hoops just to file the paperwork and pay the fees that the process was clearly intended to be obstructive. Then you had to wait at least six months for the permit. The law in my state says they have to be issued within 30 days, but they don't care. They file the request under "they'll forget about it after six months" and delay and delay and delay. A call reminding them of their own state laws may create some small motion in the process—or mark you as a troublemaker. In the county I live in now, the process requires two separate visits to court houses and police stations, fingerprints, applications and fees which take a few hours, but the license—if you are eligible—comes in about one month. Deliberate obstruction is usually a local matter and you may just have to grin and bear it while they try to keep you from your constitutional rights.

In most cases, a person unfamiliar with firearms will purchase a firearm locally. If you are not an experienced and capable firearm owner already, you should rely on the advice of your instructor and the available products when purchasing trigger locks or gun safes. You will also need ammunition for whatever firearm you buy. Think ahead and purchase additional ammunition, especially for common weapons like rifles or shotguns, to use as barter.

(DISCLAIMER: The information found within is not legal advice, nor legal interpretation of the federal or state gun laws in effect at the time of print, and any actions or inactions the reader takes are their own. Neither Solutions From Science nor the author are liable for any interpretation or action on the part of the reader.)

SECTION 4.1: SECURITY 3-5-7 TRACK

Goal: To protect yourself and your family from intruders during a short-term emergency.

Many of the items listed in the General Information section will stand you in good stead in a short-term emergency, especially the battery-powered items in the case of no electricity. They may allow you to flee or at least scare the intruders off.

What To Do

If you are unwilling to purchase and learn how to safely handle a firearm, then go to the www.thehomesecuritysuperstore.com (or a similar website or store) and investigate their products. Select those that fit your needs, order, and install them.

That's it!! You're done with 3-5-7.

SECTION 4.2: SECURITY FEND TRACK

Goal: To defend yourself or your family in the event that a police presence is erratic, slow, or unavailable for periods of time.

In a long-term FEND or OTG situation, without a strong police presence or one in which it is erratic or slow to respond, you and your family are vulnerable if you refuse to purchase a firearm and learn how to use it properly and safely. In these situations, the criminals may be opportunists that flee at the first sign their criminal career might be ended by something you have installed to protect your home. Or they may be true monsters who don't blink an eye at inflicting carnage, and to whom murder, rape and torture is a blood sport. If you have something they want—even a can of beans—they might kill you for it. In a serious civilization breakdown, they may run in gangs, not alone or paired.

There is a resource for those who are dedicated to protecting their family. It is called *Home Defense Tactics* from www.HomeDefenseTactics.com. It teaches you how to protect yourself, with or without a gun, in extremely dangerous home-invasion situations. It also helps you assess your home's security weaknesses as seen through the eyes of a home invader, offers real solutions for making your home less vulnerable, and helps you plan an escape route. If you are one of those people who cry when they vacuum up dust bunnies, or who get squeamish even looking at pictures of guns, you may want to avoid this book because it will ruin your whole day. But even without the weapons information, it is still well-worth the price of about $60 because it covers a lot of other practical ways to fight back without a gun as well. It is completely unique.

If you do purchase a firearm, you should:

- ☑ Take a gun safety class before purchasing the fire arm.

- ☑ Practice, practice, practice.

- ☑ Secure the firearm in a safe or in another manner against unauthorized use or theft.

- ☑ Scrupulously obey all local laws and regulations and be aware of the state of self-defense actions in your state.

Once again, you might encounter a time when you have to take steps to hide your guns. Sam Adam's *Hide Your Guns* offers useful strategies for hiding firearms. You can get it at www.hideyourguns.com for $50 in audio or print form.

SECTION 4.3: SECURITY OTG TRACK

Goal: The same as FEND, but you are on your own. The police and justice system is non-existent and the time period is indefinite.

There isn't much more to add, as you are either equipped, trained, experienced, and willing to defend your family, or you are not. In an OTG world, being able to defend yourself could mean the difference between life and death for your entire family.

ECONOMICS/ FINANCES

. . . a government big enough to give you everything you want is a government big enough to take from you everything you have.

~President Gerald Ford, August 12, 1974 ~

5

Chapter

There is a knock on the door. Two men in dark suits are standing on your doorstep. They introduce themselves as Special Agents Tom Smith and Jerry Jones of the Consumer Financial Protection Oversight Bureau of the federal government.

Agent Smith: Good morning, Miz Adams. How are you? We're from the government and we're here to help. May we come in? Oh, silly me, of course we can come in.

Agent Jones: We came to talk to you today about your bank account. You know, of course, that your bank monitors your account for irregularities. It's for your own protection. Well, your bank has informed us that your account has some issues. We've reviewed it and find that in the last year, about once a month, you removed a significant amount of cash from your savings account. That concerns us. You may not realize how safe our banking and currency system is and how dangerous it is to keep cash on hand. Could you tell us what you did with it? Do you still have it?

Excuse me? It's your money, you paid your taxes, you can do whatever you want with it! (Special Agents Tom and Jerry look at each other significantly and smile. "Her money...ha ha ha ha.")

Agent Smith: Sorry, just an inside joke. Now, Miz Adams, what did you do with it? It seems to us that you might think our banking system isn't as safe as our Leader says it is. That would be wrong-headed, of course. Everything is fine. The government tells us so every day. Do you still have it? If you don't, can you show us receipts about how you spent it? Well, actually . . . we've had a little tip that you bought quite a lot of wheat seeds for cash in the last few months. We have also noted that you recently bought some gold of which you have taken possession. Is that true? If it is, that might show you don't trust our financial system as completely as a Good Citizen should. The Leader's recent Emergency Recovery Executive Order frowns on that kind of doubt. You will, of course, give us permission to search your house. Oh, wait, we don't need permission under the Emergency Recovery Executive Order. Please step outside.

Don't think that could happen? Here are the laws and regulations in effect now— that we know of—about what you can do with your own money without someone taking an interest in your activities:

The **Bank Secrecy Act of 1970 (BSA)** <u>requires financial institutions in the United States to assist U.S. government agencies</u> to detect and prevent money laundering. Specifically, they must keep records of cash purchases of negotiable instruments and <u>file reports</u> of cash purchases of $10,000 or more that might signify money laundering, tax evasion, or <u>other criminal activities</u>. That sounds noble, doesn't it? Who wouldn't want to stop drug dealers and criminals from laundering their money? Not me.

But wait, it turns out that they have to report <u>multiple</u> currency transactions as a <u>single</u> transaction if they are: (a) conducted by or on behalf of the same person, and (b) they result in cash received or <u>disbursed</u> by the financial institution of more than $10,000 on the same day. (FinCEN Form 104 Currency Transaction Report [CTR]).

Banks must also report "<u>any suspicious transaction relevant to a possible violation of law or regulation.</u>" (Treasury Department Form 99-22.47 and OCC Form 8010-1 Suspicious Activity Report [SAR].)   The banks are specifically told that the customer must NOT be informed that a SAR is being filed with the Financial Crimes Enforcement Network. *Any suspicious transaction?* What is a "suspicious" transaction? Withdrawing your own money? A "possible violation" of a "law or regulation." Which laws and regulations, exactly?

The banks have to file a form every two years that exempts businesses from being busted for conducting common business operations like payrolls or cash income from a restaurant or bar. Further, any business receiving one or more related cash payments totaling $10,000 or more must file Form 8300.

The punishment for not reporting is extremely high fines and long prison sentences for the individual and/or the banking institution.

The bank reports the individual's bank account number, name, address, and social security number. Software companies have developed applications to monitor bank customer transactions on a daily basis and using customer historical information and account profiling, they provide a "whole picture" to the bank management. Transaction monitoring can include <u>cash deposits and withdrawals</u>, wire transfers and ACH activity.

The Patriot Act, Title III, updated and reinforced this act. Again, it's in the name of a noble cause—rooting out the financial support of terrorism. But what will be defined as "terrorism," or in government-speak, "man-caused disasters," in the future? A political dissident? An independent-minded patriot?

And don't think you can make income offshore or store any income offshore without the government knowing. Any signatory interest in an offshore banking account must be disclosed on your income tax form and appropriate taxes paid. Some feel that the disclosure of offshore bank accounts is enough to trigger an automatic audit. So much for staying "under the radar".

That's just what we know they can do from the public domain. What they actually do quietly would probably cause your hair to stand straight up and turn white. The way our laws and regulatory system are heading, there will be <u>nothing</u> private about any of our finances in the future. Therefore, it is necessary to assume that withdrawing a significant amount of cash, relative to your income or savings, on a regular basis, will be flagged at the bank. Although your transactions probably won't fall into the $10,000 per day range and therefore won't automatically be reported to the feds, it is not beyond the pale that the government could request and get the banking information on anyone they choose to target, based upon the flimsiest of suspicions or in the interests of "national security."

Unfortunately, this is the modern world and you can't avoid using debit and credit cards, but you can stay under the radar as much as possible and try to avoid significantly tripping any of their triggers. Work hard at keeping your overall prepping activities under cover. If possible, you should shop locally and use cash where possible for "suspicious" activities, such as buying large amounts of grain or legumes, or similar large prepping purchases. However, as you may have noticed, most of your purchases are going to be placed through the Internet, for instance at Amazon – The Super Prepper's Store (ASPS). One look at your debit or credit card purchases on Amazon alone and you will be busted. You will probably be able to get away with why you need a closet full of toilet paper by telling them that you have a phobia about running out of toilet paper and besides, it was on sale, but you won't be able to get away with that in regard to the purchase of a closet full of big buckets of grain or a year's stock of freeze-dried food.

Chapter 5

SECTION 5.1:
ECONOMICS/FINANCES 3-5-7 TRACK

Goal: To have some cash on hand for emergencies in case the bank is closed for a period of time and you can't access your accounts.

In general, it is recommended that you should keep some cash on hand for emergencies should the bank be physically closed and/or other access to accounts restricted. You may need it to provide for yourself during an evacuation, or to tide you over when trying to buy food or gas or pay important bills without access to your bank account for a short time.

If you choose to store cash in your home, you must do two things:

☑ Tell **NO ONE**, other than another responsible adult in your immediate family, that you have cash in your home. DO NOT tell your younger children, who may talk about it unwittingly and put you and your family in danger. With older children, if they are aware of the cash, stress the <u>need for silence</u> in this matter.

☑ Get a fire-proof safe. These safes are available at any office supply store. Most are not large, especially when you open them and find the fire-proofing has eaten up a large amount of the interior space, so you may need more than one. Having a fireproof safe is just general common sense. You should keep your important papers, passports, assets, etc. in them. Then HIDE the safe(s). Put the keys in a non-related, secure-but-easily-accessible place. Never mind Special Agents Tom and Jerry. You need to protect an easily portable item that contains ALL your information and current liquid assets from being picked up and toted out by a common burglar.

☑ Alternatives for hiding cash (if you don't mind if it might be destroyed in a fire) include fake cans (beer, pop, pet food, and AJAX cans, among others), hollowed out books, wall safes behind clocks and closet lights, wall plugs, and surge protectors.

TIP:
You can also hide your small valuables inside a real bottle of Dasani water. The hiding place is behind the label, but the top and the bottom of the bottle is filled with water. It is amazing! It looks and feels just like a bottle of water. It is available from www.thehomesecuritysuperstore. com

For the 3-5-7 track, this generally all you need to do. Just do it SAFELY and QUIETLY.

SECTION 5.2:
ECONOMICS/FINANCES FEND TRACK

Goal: To have some backup to paper money.

In the FEND track, besides deepening your cash reserve, you might want to consider acquiring precious metals such as gold and silver, as a hedge against inflation or currency collapse. At this point a caveat is necessary: <u>I am not a qualified investment advisor and therefore cannot legally offer financial investment advice</u>. Everyone's financial situation is different and you would be a total fool to do anything based on something I, um . . . heard was a good idea. On the other hand, I've heard a few tips that might help <u>should you</u>, after <u>careful research</u> and being <u>fully aware of the risks</u>, decide to acquire precious metals <u>completely on your own</u>, of course. Got it?

There are many ways to acquire interests in precious metals, including gold-backed IRAs, buying precious metals and warehousing them elsewhere, investing in them on the commodities market, or purchasing them from reputable dealers on the Internet, or even on eBay. These are investment matters about which I am completely unqualified to even speak, never mind advise someone. They are also outside the scope of this guide. Should you decide to invest in any of these or any other financial product, it is your responsibility to find a qualified and capable investment expert, do your homework, and make the decision that is best for you with full knowledge of the risk.

Gold Confiscation—Could It Happen Again?

Most of us have heard what happened to gold in 1933. The dollar was collapsing and the feds didn't have enough gold in the Treasury to back it. (Many think we have very little gold stock today either, but no one can find out because it's a really, really big secret.) President Roosevelt issued Executive Order No. 6073, which ordered the confiscation of all private gold. A paper certificate was then issued for the value of the confiscated gold which was set at $20 an ounce. Then the price of gold was reset to $35 and the government pocketed the difference. Shortly after that the government devalued paper currency by 40%. Oops. Guess who lost their shirt? (Tip: Not Uncle Sam.) The penalty was a very steep fine or ten years in jail if you forgot to turn your gold in. The ban on owning gold wasn't removed until August 15, 1974.

Rare collectible gold coins were exempted from confiscation because it would have been a logistical nightmare to value them on a coin-by-coin basis. Strangely, the government also left silver alone.

The best way that I've, um . . . heard for acquiring physical gold or silver is to buy it quietly from a local dealer. I have heard that the following guidelines are sensible:

☑ Locate a precious metals dealer in your community. This is not the shop whose sign blinks "WE BUY GOLD" in big neon letters where you take your gold chains and get money for them. This must be a reputable dealer that sells physical gold or silver. You may need to make a few calls to find the right one. If the place is locked up like Fort Knox overnight, there are security cameras everywhere, and the sales people are armed, you are probably in the right place. These people are serious and know their business, and while you are in there, you are safer than in a police station.

☑ If you intend to buy significant amounts of gold or silver, you might want to contact the dealer before just turning up. Precious metals go through periods of scarcity and they may not have the stock on hand.

☑ Buy it in cash and take possession of it. Buying in cash usually means that you will receive a receipt without your name on it. Don't offer them your name either—it's best just to be business buddies in this case. Their business records will be among the first seized if the government decides to confiscate gold, and the feds will be very interested in anyone who bought gold or silver on the record. Stay under the radar. Buy in small quantities over a period of time and pay in cash.

☑ Keep the receipt(s) in your fireproof safe because it lists the price at which you bought it. If you sell it formally in the future, you will need the receipt to prove the capital gains you realized on it for your taxes. ALWAYS be completely straight with the IRS. Give them NO excuse to look at you twice—or even once for that matter.

☑ Be aware that starting in 2012, any sale/purchase over $600 must be recorded on a 1099-Misc form. That is, if you buy $601 dollars of silver YOU must issue the dealer a 1099-Misc form which HE has to file with his taxes just in case he was about to forget to put your purchase on his taxable income.

Part of this law is the feds agonizing over unreported taxable income conducted in cash, but another reason is a real attempt to control the sales of gold without having to identify yourself. Starting in 2012, you will not be able to buy gold (about $1,300 an ounce in October 2010) without having to issue a 1099-Misc to the dealer. Silver (about $22) could still be purchased quietly—at least at today's prices.

TIP:
As of December 2010, Congress is currently talking about repealing the 1099 provision in the health care bill. Whether that happens or not is anybody's guess and it would be unwise to count on it.

☑ A silver or gold coin is a truly beautiful thing and gives real meaning to the concept of "intrinsic value." Our legal tender is rubbishy bits of paper and collections of discount metals painted a silver color, which the government SAYS is worth something because, er... they say it is. Weigh a silver 1-ounce coin in your hand against a couple of today's quarters and the comparison will make you sick at heart with worry about the value of our money. There's a reason gold and silver were the prerogatives of kings and are called "precious metals." They are transcendent just in their very existence.

☑ Both silver and gold are sold as modern minted coins, rare coins or collectibles, or in solid ingots of various sizes. Silver is also sold as "face," that is, bags of quarters, dimes, and half dollars minted before 1965. You can still find some of these coins in circulation today, but it is very rare indeed.

☑ You could buy collectible gold and silver, but obviously you will be paying far more than the value of the actual precious metal in the item. On the other hand, it probably won't be confiscated and then what will it be worth in the "New World"? It would be priceless—literally. Collectible silver and gold is outside the scope of this guide. If you want to invest in collectible gold or silver, you will have to find a good, honest broker or learn your subject first, because this is a complex form of investment.

What follows is about silver, which is called the "poor man's gold" for a good reason:

☑ Silver coins can be official U.S. minted money—such as Silver Eagles—or they can be minted privately. The privately minted coins are not legal tender but they are still 99.99% pure silver.

☑ In 1964 the United States went off the gold standard, and all coins after that were made of rubbish metals painted silver. Coinage before 1965 was made up of 90% silver and 10% copper. You can tell the difference by looking at the edges. The pre-1965 coins are all silver, but the modern coins have an orange filling that is highly obvious and trashy looking. Pre-1965 coins can be bought in units called "face." "Face" is not half as beautiful as the gorgeous silver one-ounce coins—it's just beat up old nickels, dimes and quarters—but each coin is worth far more than 5, 10 or 25 cents at current silver values. In a barter economy, they will be far more useful than big coins. Since they are legal U.S. tender, you could—if you went temporarily crazy—spend them like actual pocket change.

If you want to know what the "melt value" of a pre-1965 quarter is at any given time, you can use this formula:

1. Calculate the value of the silver in the quarter:

Silver price today x .90 x 6.25 (total weight in grams) x .0321507466 (ounce/gram conversion factor)

2. Calculate the value of the copper in the quarter:

Copper price today x .10 (10%) x 6.25 x .00220462262 (copper's ounce/ gram conversion factor)

3. Add them up.

Let's say silver is at $22 (which it is very near) and copper is at $3.50.

☑ The silver in the quarter is worth $3.97.
☑ The copper in the quarter is worth .004 cents.

Not much adding to do here, your quarter is worth $3.97. Now imagine if silver was valued at $300 per ounce (or one minted silver coin). That one grungy quarter would be worth nearly $55.

In a barter world, it is the mobility and perceived value of the coins that matters. If the financial system did break down entirely, a new currency standard could well become barter or this type of silver.

☑ If you buy a minted one-ounce silver coin, you will pay the spot price (the exact amount that silver is selling for at the time of your purchase) plus a minting cost and a dealer's handling cost. The two additional costs usually come to between $2 and $3 per coin, but it varies with the dealer.

☑ Face is a little more complicated. A $1,000 face bag of dimes, for instance, contains 10,000 actual dimes. 10,000 dimes add up to $1,000 at their face value of 10 cents apiece—thus the name "$1,000 face" bag. However, 10,000 pre-1965 dimes actually contain 715 ounces of pure silver. Face sells for less than the comparable amount of silver in the form of one-ounce silver coins because there is no minting fee. Therefore, you can buy more silver for your money in face bags. Today (October 2010) a $1,000 face bag of Roosevelt dimes is selling for $15.84 per $1 face, or $15,840 for 10,000 dimes. A single one-ounce silver coin was selling for $21.17. It isn't an exact correlation because the coin is 99.99% silver and $1 of face is 90% silver, but you get the idea. But don't panic if you don't have $15,000. You can buy face in $250 and $500 face bags too ("quarter face" or "half face.") And if the dealer is willing, you can ask for a specific dollar amount—say $1,000 dollars worth in actual silver content. The dealer then measures out as near to $1,000 of the actual silver content on a scale as he can manage. This is where calling ahead is a real courtesy because you want to be sure they have as much face on hand as you want to buy, and then they have to measure it out. If you want a mix of quarters and dimes, it takes a little while to do because the amount of silver is different in each one and it takes a little tinkering to get to the dollar figure you want to buy. Not every dealer will measure out partial amounts of face for you, however, so it is best to ask ahead of time. If they won't measure out partial amounts, you will have to buy the quarter, half or full face they offer, or find a dealer who will.

By the time this book was published in March 2011, silver had risen to almost $35 an ounce. A $1,000 face amount of silver now costs about $24,500. A silver pre-1965 quarter is now worth about $6.30. Gold has risen as well to over $1,400 an ounce. The lesson to be learned is that if you decide that physical gold or silver has a place in your survival or investment strategies, then you should act QUICKLY, as the turmoil around the world will probably only cause higher increases in prices.

☑ Face will be more useful in a world where the currency has collapsed than a big silver coin. A few dimes or quarters can be doled out to buy something or traded for items a lot easier than a big silver coin. The silver coins can kept for emergencies where large amounts of money might be needed quickly. Unless the world is entirely broken down, you will have to redeem the coin formally and accept the taxation.

You can purchase precious metals on the Internet or from eBay. But your transaction will be on the record and Special Agents Tom and Jerry can let their fingers do the walking on their computer keyboards. They won't even have to leave the office to find you.

Where To Keep Your Precious Metals

You may wish to keep your precious metals in a safe deposit box for safety. The down side to that is you may not be able to get to it in a time of crisis if the bank is physically closed. Furthermore, I wouldn't put it past the Powers That Be to demand that safe deposit boxes be opened and searched for precious metals if they get really, really desperate. It's not the like banks are actually independent of the government any more, is it?

If you decide to take physical possession of your precious metals and keep them at home, this is where a real need for SECRECY <u>must be enforced</u>. If you buy silver or gold at today's prices and it skyrockets in value, even a small purchase of silver or gold may be worth a very great deal. Advertising you have that kind of money on hand is asking for a tragedy of epic proportions.

Remember, if you decide to keep it at home, you must **HIDE IT**. Take some time with hiding your precious metals, even more than with food. It could be the difference between life and death in a post-apocalypse world. Really get creative and devious. Serious paranoia in this matter is a fundamental requirement. It would be best to hide it around other metal objects (but not near electricity, as it is a conductor.) Book safes and fireproof safes are not even remotely serious candidates for hiding precious metals. Hide it in those obvious places and Special Agents Tom and Jerry will be strolling down your sidewalk carrying your entire net worth under their arms in short order.

 TIP:
Face can be hidden in plain sight. For instance, it can be mixed innocently with modern coins in your kid's piggy bank. Each coin would have to be examined closely to figure out what it really was. Throw in a lot of pennies and top it off with a handful of our modern junky coins so that a quick handful reveals no real silver. Since some of the silver coins are easily over 50 years old and very worn looking, it would be wise to remove them entirely and hide them somewhere else because they are very noticeable at a glance.

Write down everywhere you have hidden your precious metals in a code and put it in a file marked "Grandma's Old Recipes for Bread" (or something similar) in the back of a file drawer or in the fire proof safe. Be sure to stick a few old recipes for bread inside the file. Tell NO ONE, except a trusted life partner, or VERY good friend you would trust with your <u>life</u>, about the list and what's on it.

Finally, anything you decide to do regarding investing in precious metals should be made only after careful research, responsible analysis of your financial situation, and a sober evaluation of the risks. If the value of gold and silver drops to one cent an ounce tomorrow, you made the decision and you alone are responsible for the consequences.

Should the moment ever come when we are ordered to turn in our gold or silver to the feds, anyone who has invested in precious metals will have an agonizing decision to make, and the consequences are yours alone. We don't claim to be financial consultants by any means, so you should always consult a licensed financial advisor before making any decisions.

SECTION 5.3:
ECONOMICS/FINANCES OTG TRACK

Goal: To have financial resources with which you can barter or pay in the "New World."

Get more precious metals, especially face. In OTG you can use your cash stash to light a fire in the fireplace.

That's it.

COMMUNICATIONS

We've arranged a civilization in which most crucial elements profoundly depend on science and technology.

- Carl Sagan -

6

Chapter

It's a clear beautiful Sunday evening in the early fall. You close the lid of your laptop, relieved that you have finally finished your report for work tomorrow. Just then the lights flicker for a few seconds, and go off. You sigh and rummage in the junk drawer for your flashlight and, when you can't find it, you grab a decorative candle and light it. You figure you might as well go to bed early. As you get ready for bed, you glance outside at a strangely-darkened street and you notice that the sky is rippling with a curtain of colored lights. It's beautiful, but after you have crawled into bed, you uneasily watch the sky through the window. It's unusual, sure, but there's no real reason to believe that the power won't be back on by morning and your world will begin to turn again.

But when you get up in the morning, there's still no electricity. You try to call work on your cell phone to find out if they have power and if there is any point to coming in right now, only to find that the phone isn't working. You throw it on the counter and turn on the tap to fill a pot to make coffee and then, just as you remember there's not going to be any coffee this morning, the water from the faucet sputters and stops.

You can't find out what happened from the TV so you power up your laptop and try to get onto the Internet, hoping that the fact that it is wireless will make a difference. It doesn't. No Internet. You try the battery-powered radio and search for local news stations, but there's only static. Now you start to worry. Clearly, this is not a normal power outage. As you stand in your kitchen, confused, you know something is very wrong, but you have no idea how to find out what happened, how long it will last, or what you should do.

You were right. It isn't a normal power outage. You were so busy over the weekend working on your report that you missed a small item that barely registered on the Internet, radio or TV: NASA scientists had observed that the sun had just ejected a giant fireball (called a CME, or "Coronal Mass Ejection") from its surface. They had warned there would be beautiful auroras in various places around the world and possibly some interference with communications depending on where you lived, but ultimately they didn't think it would be much more than a nuisance. The scientists were wrong.

CMEs are large clouds of charged particles (plasma) that are ejected from the sun and speed through space at speeds as high as a million miles an hour. When the plasma cloud interacts with the atmosphere of the Earth, it causes a geomagnetic storm that can affect the electrical grid and foul up communication networks. Solar flares are not uncommon and usually occur during years of high sun-spot activity (a period of time we are coming up on now), but not always. Most of them just deal Earth a glancing blow or don't even interact with Earth at all. Even if they do affect us, they cause only minor trouble. But a strong CME, solidly on an interception course with the Earth, can melt the key points in the electrical grid beyond immediate repair. Although we can see these flares erupt on the surface of the sun, we don't know how strong they are going to be until they get very near Earth. Then there are only seconds left before it hits.

This is not just speculation. There are precedents for a large CME event, for instance, the "Carrington Event" (named for the British astronomer, Richard Carrington, who first spotted the large flare) that occurred in September 1859. It only took 18 hours to get to the Earth, which was unusual because such a journey should normally have taken three to four days. In 1859 there was no electrical grid, but the CME did cause telegraph networks to fail all over Europe and North America. Telegraph paper spontaneously caught fire and some telegraph systems appeared to continue to send and receive messages despite having been disconnected from their power supplies.

Closer to today, in March 1989, the entire province of Quebec, Ontario went dark in an elapsed time of 90 seconds. The storm lasted for about 26 hours and the blackout came very close to extending into the United States, all down the east coast and across the Pacific Northwest. Satellites over the pole lost control for several hours. Fortunately, it was a relatively weak CME and the damage was contained because the power surge tripped the circuit breakers on the power grid instead of just frying them totally. Altogether the blackout lasted nine hours and affected nearly six million people. In August 1989, another geomagnetic storm affected microchips and led to a halt of all trading on Toronto's stock exchange.

The Carrington Event was the strongest documented geomagnetic storm to date. The September 1989 event was less than 1/10 the size of the Carrington Event. There have been others, including a large one in 2003, in which the Earth just barely dodged the bullet.

Our electrical power grid is highly complex and intricately connected. A large CME could literally melt the transformer hubs at the heart of our power grid. The damage could take four to ten years to fix because these units are huge, complex to make, difficult to transport—and made in China.

What you do not know as you stand in your kitchen, puzzled, is that the economy has crashed, your drinkable water has ceased to exist, the sewage system is no longer working, hospitals will be out of business within three days when their generators run out of fuel, life-maintaining medicines will be unavailable, grocery stores will be empty before the day is over, and you won't be watching TV or listening to most radios for a long time to come. By the time you figure it out, you will be inexorably behind the survival curve.

GENERAL INFORMATION

Everyone Needs a Good Radio

Any radio you purchase in the future should be powered by batteries, if possible. Regular batteries, of course, have a limited life and must be discarded after they are exhausted. In order to provide battery power for the extended future you need to purchase:

- ☑ <u>High Capacity NiMH Rechargeable batteries</u>. You should get a stock of AA, AAA, C, D and 9V.

- ☑ An <u>electric battery charger</u> for all the battery sizes (although most of them don't have 9V capacity, which isn't a deal breaker.)

- ☑ A <u>solar-powered battery charger</u> in case there is no electricity—which is precisely when, after all, you need batteries.

Shopping for Re-Chargeable Batteries

It is a bad idea to purchase batteries of any kind from department, retail, or office supply stores. You will pay through the nose for them. The only exception is when there is a 2-for-1 sale, then you at least get close to the cost of batteries ordered from the Internet.

- ☑ At this time on www.all-battery.com, you can order a 34-piece rechargeable battery supply that contains all five sizes (AA, AAA, C, D, and 9V) for about $70. The full cost in a retail store would be about $170. Get two packs if you can so one set can be recharging and the other in use.

There are many sources on the Internet for NiMH batteries and some shopping around will save you a lot of money.

Battery Chargers

Electric battery chargers range across the price spectrum from $20 to hundreds of dollars. Purchase the best you can afford. Be sure to get one with the ability to hold at least AA, AAA, C, and D batteries, and which charges them in the quickest amount of time. The All-Battery site offers many different kinds of electric battery chargers.

Finally, you should invest in:

☑ A solar battery charger. If budget is an issue, skip the electric charger for now and buy the solar charger. You can always go back and fill in your battery charging needs with an electric charger later. Silicon Solar offers a solar battery charger that covers AA, AAA, C, and D and costs $20. (Product number 04-1142 at http://www.siliconsolar.com/solar-battery-charger-aa-aaa-c-and-d-p-135.html.) Of course, you will need the sun and it will take longer than electric recharging, but you are independent of electricity.

☑ A solar charger for mobile devices (i.e. cell phones, MP3 players, etc.) The REI website (www.rei.com) sells an item from Highgear called the Solarpod (Model 10073, Item number 799-010-0013) with connector cables and 8 adaptor tips. The solar charging unit is about the size of a deck of cards. With this you can keep your cell phone and other electronic items charged in case of a power outage. It costs about $50.

While we will all curse the loss of our continuous contact with the world—and many will go into actual withdrawal—it is worthwhile to consider the benefits of quiet. The truth is our lives are filled to the brim with noise pollution. Around silence comes wisdom. And no . . . there's no app for that. A few days of no computer games, 24-hour television, Twittering, networking, texting, jabbering on the cell phone, email, and surfing the web may not be all that awful. You might discover you have a family again and a deck of cards or a Monopoly game might be a life saver.

Using the Forms

☑ Set up a **Shopping List** for **Communications Equipment** (Appendix B).

☑ After you have purchased the items, erase them from the **Shopping List** and transfer them to the **Inventory Form** (Appendix C.)

SECTION 6.1:
COMMUNICATIONS 3-5-7 TRACK

Goal : To be able to communicate with your family to share emergency instructions and to be able to get extreme weather or evacuation information.

Establishing a Contact Plan

In the event of an emergency, you will need to be able to get in touch with your family immediately. Therefore everyone needs to be provided with cell phones. Everyone should be given a primary contact number. If that person is not available or inaccessible, everyone should have a second contact number for another adult, preferably outside the area, who can relay instructions. You should set up a safe meeting point, other than your home, where people can meet, with or without instructions, if they cannot get home.

TIP:
It would be worthwhile to keep one telephone land line in the event cell phones, the Internet, or email are unusable, as there is a possibility that land lines may still work.

Radios

Other than establishing a plan of contact for your family members, the only thing you need for the 3-5-7 track is a good weather radio. It can be electric, but it should also be able to run on batteries or have a solar-charging capacity in the event of an extended power outage. Some weather radios can be charged by cranking a little handle in case the radio can't be solar charged readily.

Weather radios are plentiful and readily available in stores and all over the Internet. They are inexpensive, running between $30 and $40.

TIP:
It would also be wise to invest in a small radio with a weather channel for your Go-Bag.

What to Get For 3-5-7

☑ Set up your entire family with cell phones for emergency communications.

☑ Purchase a good weather radio that runs on batteries, solar power or a crank.

That's it! You are ready for 3-5-7.

SECTION 6.2:
COMMUNICATIONS FEND TRACK

Goals: To be able to find or keep up with news of events in your area or region even if most sources of information are not accessible.

Shortwave Radios

Should you have a secret yen to listen to Radio RSA (Johannesburg, South Africa), Radio Malaysia (Kuala Lumpur, Malaysia), Radio Norway (Oslo, Norway), Radio Iran (Teheran, Iran), Radio New Zealand (Wellington, New Zealand), BBC London (London, England), or Voice of Greece (Athens, Greece), you are in luck! You can do that with a shortwave radio. Besides being fascinating in itself to poke around the shortwave radio spectrum, if your region (or even the whole country) experienced an Internet or other communications blackout, so long as the radio was still working (i.e. not electronically fried) you would be able to access some kind of news on the situation—even if it does come from China or Iran. (Or maybe especially if it <u>does </u>come from China or Iran!)

Shortwave radios are only receivers. You cannot broadcast on them as you can on CB radios and ham radios. CB and ham radios requires require antennas and a lot of time and equipment, and are not considered in this guide.

On the <u>plus</u> side, shortwave radios can be used in situations where Internet and satellite communications service is unavailable. Another bonus is that shortwave radio is difficult to censor by authorities since most stations originate outside their control.

On the <u>negative</u> side, shortwave radio reception is affected by the distance from the transmitter, the time of day, and solar activity, which can interfere with the ionosphere and keep it from reflecting shortwave radio frequencies.

TIP:
In the event of a strong geomagnetic storm, it may be a little while before you can get stations clearly from other parts of the world to find out what might be happening in your part of the world. Eventually, however, a shortwave radio may be the only way to establish contact with some place far away that is not similarly or as badly affected.

I recommend the Sangean ATS 505P. It gets AM, FM, shortwave and SSB (single sideband reception). It has a nice carrying case, a long portable shortwave antenna, and earbuds. It has a keypad for direct station entry and 45 memory presets. It has an AC adaptor, but runs on four "AA" batteries in a pinch. You can get this radio at C. Crane, www.ccrane.com, for $120. Their customer service is excellent if you have questions.

Shortwave radio stations broadcast at different times of the day and on different frequencies. You should get on the Internet and print out basic information on the stations, when and where they are available, and then experiment. A very good start is:

☑   http://support.radioshack.com/support_electronics/doc66/66356.htm or

☑   "Introduction to Shortwave Listening" at http://www.dxing.com/swlinto. htm

You might want to find and print this information before there is no Internet or access to it is limited.

TIP:
You can get addicted to twiddling with a shortwave radio. The first time I got the UN station out of China, it just knocked my socks off. However, keep in mind you have many things to do right now. Save your radio station browsing for later and enjoy!

What to Get for the FEND Track

☑   A shortwave radio.

☑   A weather radio.

☑   A good supply of rechargeable batteries.

☑   An electric recharger (if the power is on) and a solar recharger for when it is not.

That's it!!! You are done with FEND.

SECTION 6.3:
COMMUNICATIONS OTG TRACK

Goal: In the event of a major catastrophe, to be able get some news from the outside world—even if it is from Europe or Russia. If it's that big, they'll be talking about it.

As in the FEND track, you will need a weather radio and a shortwave radio.

An Important Internet Tip

In the event the Powers That Be decide the Internet is allowing access to Too Much Information, and they really need to restrict it so we don't get All Confused with Facts and Other Dangerous Information, you should do the following:

- ☑ While you still have the Internet, go to www.cqcounter.com/whois/.

- ☑ Put in the domain name(s) for any website(s) you depend on for vital information. The domain name is the name you type in on the Internet access bar. (Example: www.domainname.com.)

- ☑ They will give you a lot of information on that domain name but the most important is the IP address. It will be a series of numbers with periods between them. (Example: 111.111.11.111)

- ☑ Print out that information for all websites of interest to you and keep it safe.

With the IP address, in the event the Powers That Be censor or restrict Internet service providers, it <u>may</u> still be possible to access the website using the numerical IP address. But it is worth considering that it will take the PTB about a nanosecond to figure out that you might be Thwarting Their Will and Learning Stuff by using IP addresses. This is a situation where your 11-year-old computer genius might come in handy. Food for thought.

You're welcome!

What to Get for OTG

- ☑ A weather radio
- ☑ The Sangean 505P or a similar shortwave radio
- ☑ A good supply of rechargeable batteries
- ☑ A solar-powered battery recharger

Finally, you should prepare for the possible restriction of the Internet by collecting IP addresses.

That's it!!! You're done for the OTG track.

HEATING, COOLING, LIGHTING, AND COOKING

If the world is cold, make it your business to build fires.

- Horace Traubel -

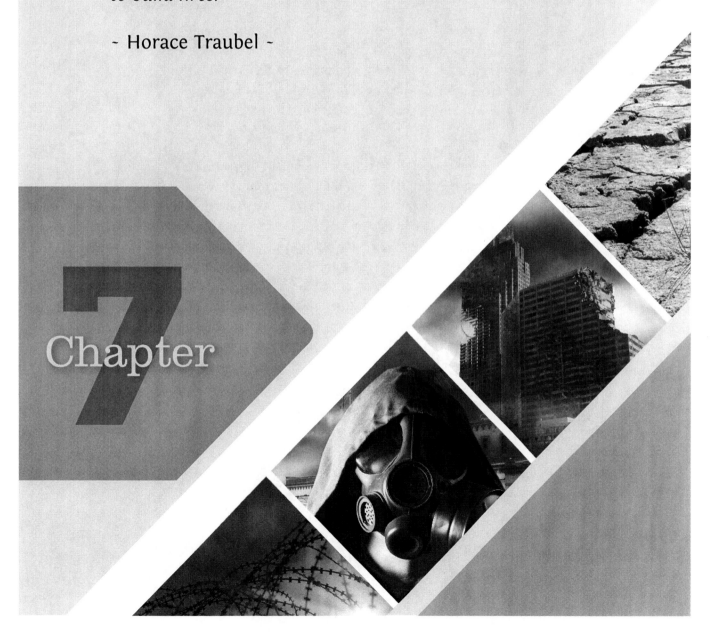

Chapter

7

A Category 3 hurricane smashes through your region. You evacuate and when you return you find, thankfully, that your house is still standing, although it is a little beat up. You move back in after rigging up a few tarps and making some rough repairs and wait for the insurance man to show up. In the meantime, perhaps for several weeks, or—if you are unlucky—several months, you will need to cook, heat and/or cool your home (although the cooling part might be done for you—see the above-mentioned tarps), and get around at night without falling over the furniture.

After Hurricane Andrew hit Florida in 1993, the area looked like a "war zone." Thus began the endless and frustrating struggle with the insurance people, the government, and the utility companies to get normal life restored. The journey back to normalcy was long and hard. Not for nothing did people wear T-shirts reading, "I survived Andrew, but the recovery is killing me."

It was the same after Hurricane Ike hit the Texas coast in September 2008 and 2.6 million households were left without power. (I still have my T-shirt from that one: "I didn't like Ike.") Some 25 to 30 percent of the transmission lines were knocked down. The repairs were estimated to take, at minimum, several weeks. After Hurricane Katrina in 2005, the authorities admitted, "We can't even estimate when restoration of power will begin in St. Tammany Parish." It wasn't just the lights, but the sewers and water systems that were damaged as well. Weeks or months are a v-e-e-r-y long time if you can't cook, see at night, have clean water to drink, or be able to use the bathroom.

GENERAL INFORMATION

Any of us who have lived long enough have had to deal with the temporary loss of utilities, usually due to storms or other occurrences. You will have to plan for:

- ☑ Cooking food
- ☑ Heating and/or cooling
- ☑ Lighting

Power From the Sun Not the Utility Company

One item that you might want to consider for dealing with any power outage is a portable solar generator. This system has three components: a generator backup, a high efficiency solar panel, and a charge controller. It can be set up in just a few minutes and weighs only 65 lbs. You can recharge phones, run shortwave radios, TVs, lights, fans, and computers, as well as kitchen appliances. You can also take it with you if you have to evacuate. Unlike gas generators, there is no noise, no fumes, no maintenance and no fuel required. You can read about it at www. mysolarbackup.com. At this writing, it costs $1697 plus shipping and handling. There are a limited number available so, if you are interested, "first come, first serve" might be the best strategy.

Power From Regular Generators

Selecting and purchasing a generator is outside the scope of this guide. Obviously, those who have, or are going to purchase, a gas generator will need a stock of fuel for them and a few common replacement parts.

A Wood Stove

If you own your own home, you may want to install a small wood stove in a common or heavily used room, such as the kitchen. This also is outside the scope of this guide and, in most cases, will require an expert to install it properly and safely.

Obviously, where you live is the deciding factor in how you prepare for replacing a heating/cooling system. If you live in southern California, you may not freeze to death in the winter without power, but instead have to suffer through appalling heat and/or humidity that is equally as uncomfortable—and possibly deadly. Most of us will have to put up with a little of both at different times of the year.

For those of us that have to go with less expensive options, we will take each of the systems in turn for each track.

Using the Forms

☑ Set up a **Shopping List** for items relating to heating, cooling, lighting, and cooking (Appendix B).

☑ After you have purchased the items, erase them from the **Shopping List** and transfer them to the **Inventory Form** (Appendix C.)

SECTION 7.1: UTILITIES 3-5-7 TRACK

Goal: To muddle through a short-term emergency until the utilities are restored.

Cooking

In a 3-5-7 situation, you can get by without cooking or by temporarily using your outdoor grill. If you lose power, you have to quickly eat up what you have in the refrigerator anyway. You might as well throw it on the grill and eat it. Food that is frozen can keep for a few days in the freezer if you don't open the door. After that, if you don't have access to a solar generator or can't can what's in there, you'll have to throw it out. After the food in the refrigerator and freezer is gone, you can eat your way through what is in your cupboards.

Putting in a small store of canned goods and easy-to-prepare dried foods will keep you from having to rush out and find scarce food after about three or four days. More importantly, if there are those who may need special food or nutrition (infants, pregnant women, elderly, or persons who are sick), you should take some care in getting a basic stock of whatever they need from the first moment of the outage.

Heating/Cooling

If it is the winter and you have a real fireplace, you can have an adventure and snuggle up around it for a few days. If you don't have a fireplace, make sure you have a lot of blankets, sweaters, and thick wooly socks. With or without a fireplace, you may wish to group your activities, including sleeping, around one room and close off unnecessary rooms until the crisis is over.

TIP:
Many home fires occur at the start of the cold season as people begin to use fireplaces that haven't been cleaned for awhile. It might be wise to get your chimney professionally cleaned in the near future. You can also purchase creosote-sweeping logs, which they claim will reduce existing creosote and prevent future buildup. This product is available in supermarkets, hardware, and home improvement stores around the beginning of the cold season. They recommend using one log per season if you use your fireplace once a week, two if you use it daily and if the fire is continuous, one log every two months.

You will need to purchase a good supply of wood, not just the little seven-piece packs they sell outside the hardware or grocery store in the fall. Purchase as much as you can afford and store it under a sturdy tarp. You can also purchase fire starter logs so the fire starts smartly. Be sure you have ample matches (especially the long kind) or a clicker fire starter. Keep both out of the reach of children.

Unfortunately, there is little you can do to make your home cooler in the event of a power outage. Depending on the climate, the heat and humidity might be more uncomfortable than a few days of being chilly. A few battery-powered fans might offer a little relief.

Lighting

Flashlights

You should invest in several good flashlights and put them around the house where they can be found quickly. Those that use LED lamps are more efficient and last longer. However, the best kinds to get are ones that you can recharge by squeezing a handle or turning a crank on the flashlight.

Battery-Powered Lanterns

The camping departments of retail stores offer small battery-powered lanterns that really do provide a lot of light for their size. You can't go around with flashlights for weeks at a time, so a visit to a camping supply store or to the camping section in a department store should fix you right up.

If you like to read, you might want to purchase a small reading light so you can curl up with a book.

What to Get for 3-5-7

Cooking: Get a small stock of canned goods and dried foods. Get any special food or nutritional items required by the special needs people in your family.

Heating/Cooling: If you have a real fireplace, get some firewood stocked in, along with a lot of matches and fire starter logs. Purchase a few battery-powered fans for a little relief from the heat.

Lighting: Get flashlights and several battery-powered lanterns.

That's it!! You're done for the 3-5-7 track.

SECTION 7.2: UTILITIES FEND TRACK

Goal: To be able to deal with utilities when they are off for a longer period of time, or when there are periods of erratic functioning, scarcity, or extremely high prices.

The FEND track assumes that you may have erratic, rationed, or no utilities for periods of time. In this situation, the solar-powered generator or a regular generator may come in very handy indeed.

Here are a few things you might want to broaden or acquire if you anticipate facing a long period without utilities:

Cooking

This is where the Crisis Cooker from Solutions From Science, described in Chapter One, serves a dual purpose. This unique stove can use charcoal, wood, or propane and can be instantly set up. Its patented heat chamber conducts heat ten times more efficiently than conventional stoves. Obviously it must be used only outdoors. It is portable, weighs 26 pounds, and is made of 18-gauge steel. The price is reasonable—about $180 including shipping. The really good news is that the Crisis Cooker also satisfies your OTG cooking needs, so it is a real bargain in the end. You can read about it and order it at www.crisiscooker.com.

However, any heat source will work, including campfires, grills, or portables stoves. Portable stoves and grills are readily available from sports, camping or hiking equipment suppliers, or most department stores. However, be sure you don't buy any stove or grill that is fueled only by propane, kerosene, or white gas. You need something that can use wood or charcoal—hence the beauty of the Crisis Cooker. When the fuel is gone, so is your ability to cook food and boil water.

TIP:
Never, ever use a grill or portable camping style stove indoors.

Heating/Cooling

If you have a real fireplace, stock in as much firewood as you can afford . Make sure you have plenty of matches or fire-starting equipment. You may wish to purchase some creosote burning logs if you think you may have to use the fireplace heavily, as burning them at regular intervals will help to clean the chimney flue and prevent chimney fires.

If there is a source of wood nearby, you should consider purchasing:

☑ A chain saw, various replacement parts, and extra fuel and oil. If you are unfamiliar with chain saws, your best choice is to go to a home improvement or hardware store where you can get someone who is knowledgeable to help you choose the one that is right for you.

TIP:
You will also want to purchase extra chains in case the first one breaks. Each saw's chain is particular to it, so find someone to help you get the right one. You will also need gasoline, two-stroke oil that you mix in the gasoline, and chain bar oil. The chain bar oil keeps the chain around the bar from seizing up during use. That would be bad. Do NOT use a chainsaw without training or help, and DO wear protective clothing, strong boots, and safety glasses.

☑ An axe, maul and wedge for chopping firewood.

TIP:
A maul is a big sledge hammer that usually weighs about eight lbs. A wedge is a metal piece shaped like a big door stop. You stick it in a crack in the wood then whack it with the maul. Voila!! A piece of firewood. Also, possibly a serious injury if you have never done it before. Lifting eight pounds overhead and swinging it accurately is NOT easy. (Go ahead—lift it in the store and imagine trying to swing it not just once, but repeatedly.) Not to mention, the possibilities of cutting your foot off with an axe—which, by the way, is also not light. I hate to be sexist, but I would be perfectly willing to let a man cut my firewood in return for a portion of it. Furthermore, anytime ANYONE chops wood, they need to wear protective clothing, sturdy boots, and safety glasses.

☑ You should get a small hatchet and a simple saw for cutting up kindling, smaller trees, and branches. I saw, or chop up, medium-sized branches and fallen trees all the time with no problem.

The Internet provides a lot of information on how to safely chop wood. You should download it before there is no Internet. There is also information available about how to select the proper type of wood for burning, how different species of woods burn, and on drying the wood after it is cut.

Lighting

For lighting needs longer than a week, you should consider candles or hurricane (paraffin) lamps.

Candles

You may want to lay in a good stock of utility candles. If you use candles you must use **<u>GREAT CARE</u>**:

☑ Don't set them on a plate with a glob of wax. Seat them firmly in a sturdy container (perhaps one of those glass jars you have been saving) that will not allow them to fall over. You might want to put the candle and container inside a baking pan or on a cookie tin so that, if it does fall over, you have a chance to retrieve it before it sets the place on fire.

☑ Put them well out of the reach of children or pets.

☑ Do not put them anywhere near any combustible materials.

☑ DO NOT leave candles burning while you sleep or without attendance.

☑ Watch your clothing as you work around them.

It would be a shame to survive a catastrophe and then burn your house down, possibly killing yourself and your family. I won't even mention the possibility of destroying an entire neighborhood and threatening the lives of many others. On September 9, 2010 in Detroit, Michigan, some 85 homes burned to the ground as sparks from several fires, apparently started by power lines downed by the wind, leapt from roof to roof. It took the fire fighters 90 minutes to respond and units had to be called from suburban areas. Many of the houses were abandoned, but some houses that were destroyed were in well-tended neighborhoods. How would you feel if your dog knocked a candle off an end table and you burned down the neighborhood?

TIP:
You should have fire extinguishers on hand as a matter of course. They can be found in every hardware or home improvement store. You need the A-B-C kind that puts out most fires. The smaller ones cost about $25, but they come in larger sizes. You should have fire extinguishers on hand on every floor and, depending on the size of the house, in a number of rooms. Put them out where you can run two or three steps and grab one without searching. Forget that they might ruin your décor. A burned down house ruins your décor too. Show your children where they are and how to operate them. This is common sense. In a FEND or OTG situation where you are using candles, they are even more important.

Using candles can be dangerous!

☑ In 2003, 18,000 home fires were started by candles, resulting in 190 deaths.

☑ 34% of candle fires occurred after candles were left unattended or inadequately controlled.

☑ 26% of candle fires started because combustible materials were left by or came too close to the candle flame.

☑ 6% of candle fires were started by children.

☑ 11% of candle fires started after the candle user fell asleep.

Hurricane Lamps

A slightly better choice than candles is a hurricane lamp, or paraffin lamp. These are available in most department stores and on the Internet. The larger lamps last a long time on a single chamber of paraffin oil. The wick can be adjusted for the amount of light you want. The glass chimney around the flame provides a little protection against fire, but they can still be knocked over or off a surface, with the same—and possibly worse—result as a candle. As with candles, **BE CAREFUL**. Do not let children fiddle with the lamps and follow the same rules as with candles: watch where you put them and do not leave them unattended.

TIP:

Do not set these lamps under surfaces or near combustible materials as they emit a great deal of heat up the glass chimney. Further, they do produce fumes, so it would be wise to crack a window or door, if possible, to prevent the accumulation of toxic gases.

You will need to buy extra wicks and extra paraffin oil as well. Do not buy those little jars (about eight oz.) that most stores stock by the lamps. It will cost you a fortune to acquire a significant stock. I found 100 fl. oz. bottles at Hobby Lobby, and bought the three they had on hand. You can find the same product at http://shop.hobbylobby.com/products/ultra-pure-paraffin-lamp-oil-691717/. They are about $20 per bottle but will last forever.

TIP:

DO NOT store paraffin lamp oil where busy little hands can get at the bottles as they look like clear soda. Store them in a cool place away from any flame source.

Conserving Your Heat or Cool(er) Air

You can also take some measures to conserve your hot or cool air:

☑ Someone who is handy with a sewing machine and measuring tape can make thermal shades to hang over the windows. You can buy the material from a fabric store, or use old blankets or quilts lined on one side with emergency blankets (which are just a big square of thin foil). Sew little tabs on the top border to hang over nails or hooks, sew Velcro strips or tabs down the side and viola!—you can become a warm little mole in minutes.

Thermal curtains are laborious and tedious to make, and those with sufficient resources can pay someone to do it for them more professionally. I made my own and last year's heating bills dropped by about 1/3 since I didn't feel the need to be able to see out the windows at night or while I was at work.

TIP:
The Salvation Army or Goodwill store can help you keep costs down if you will be making these curtains yourself. You can get old blankets and quilts for a few dollars each. The emergency blankets can be bought in any department store, camping store, or from the Internet. They are quite large when rolled out. But handle them carefully as you make the curtain, as they are quite thin and flimsy. I strengthened the edges with packing tape so it wouldn't tear while I was making and using it.

☑ You might also want to buy or make door guards for the bottom of your drafty doors.

☑ You might also want to make some kind of screen for your fireplace. I made one out of Styrofoam I cadged for free from the home improvement store (they were throwing it out!! I asked for it and it was perfect!!), covered it with quilting batting, and then covered both with a piece of old curtain fabric on the front. It fits right into the fireplace hole nice and tight for the winter. You just take it away when you want to use the fireplace.

That's it for FEND!!! There is only so much you can do to keep your comfort level when the central heating and air, and lights don't work. If it lasts long enough, you will do what people everywhere have always done in tough situations—adapt.

SECTION 7.3: UTLITIES OTG TRACK

Goal: To live without any utilities for the foreseeable future.

The only thing to do for OTG is deepen your stock of the above items for the long haul, and learn how to safely use tools such as axes and chain saws.

On the bright side, I suspect that if we face long periods without electricity, we will soon start getting up when it gets light and going to bed when it gets dark. That's what our ancestors did. Think of all the sleep you'll get in the winter.

One caution: In an OTG situation, I would be very careful about showing lights or other signs of life, especially at night, until the situation stabilizes or a basic level of security returns. Even your previously-friendly neighbors might find outward displays of cooking equipment, lighting, or stockpiles of wood or other fuel very . . . attractive, if they have nothing. If you are in an area where there are a lot of people around, you may wish to keep your activities as quiet as possible and secure things like stockpiles of wood. Your thermal curtains in this case can serve as blackout curtains as well. If you want to share your resources, you want to do it on your own terms—not theirs.

HOUSEHOLD/PERSONAL HYGIENE

Without industry and frugality, nothing will do; with them, everything.

- Benjamin Franklin -

Chapter 8

The European Union finishes its slow disintegration and the world economy tanks. Our economy follows rapidly. This time the financial gods can't stop it. With lighting speed, your stock portfolio, pension, and retirement funds imitate the Hindenburg and become a big ball of flames falling out of the sky.

The feds act swiftly because a large number of people who wait for their checks to fall out of the sky regularly are going to get very, very angry very, very quickly and start breaking things—with prejudice—if they don't get their money. You? You're a different story. You are left holding those rubbishy little coins and clutching a bunch of green paper. But, wait, you say, "The federal government has to give me my money in my savings and checking accounts up to $250,000. I had $249,999 in there and I want it NOW!!" Surprise! It turns out that the federal government can't even BEGIN to cover all the money in our bank accounts. In fact, as of the end of March 2008, they held exactly 1.22% in reserve against their exposure and it's no better now. The FDIC's actual "exposure" (interesting word in this context as it kind of reminds me of the Emperor With No Clothes) is over 4.5 TRILLION dollars.

The financial geniuses, who stride across our economic landscape like gods thinking they can defy the laws of economics, decide the best thing they can do is dig the hole we are in a lot, lot deeper a lot, lot faster, and the printing presses begin to roll. They crank out the cash and throw it into the bottomless pit until the presses start smoking and melt into slag. Unfortunately, it's a little too late, as your personal finances melted into slag some time back. Oh well, everyone knows you can't make a socialist omelet unless you break a lot of your subject's nest eggs.

Welcome to the Great Depression, Supersized, Part Two. The good news is, you are now getting paid $12,000,000 an hour. The bad news is a loaf of bread costs $100,000,000—ten seconds ago. While you were reading this sentence it rose to $120,000,000. Now you get to see what your parents and/or grandparents were talking about when they told you how they had to fix the holes in their shoes with cardboard and other horror stories you thought were just quaint and sort of funny. You should have listened—you could have picked up tips. You are going to need them now.

GENERAL INFORMATION

The items in this section are not as vital to life as are the "Big Four"—Water, Food, Medicine, and Security. Clearly, not being able to find or afford to buy a bottle of Windex is not going to knock you off the survival curve, but it will help you when that bottle of Windex costs $140,000,000. Fortunately, you have two bottles in stock—so you're rich!!!! (Finally! That was a lot easier than I thought it would be!)

The basic systems you need to consider stocking up for are:

- ☑ Household supplies
- ☑ Personal hygiene supplies
- ☑ Clothing needs
- ☑ Home repair supplies
- ☑ Laundry supplies
- ☑ Sanitation and garbage issues

Shopping Tips

Most of these common items are generally available in your local department stores or direct buy stores. However, if you can bear it, you should never scorn a:

- ☑ Dollar store
- ☑ Goodwill or the Salvation Army store
- ☑ Rummage sales

It is remarkable how many basic items you can acquire in these places at a fraction of the cost of new items. Goodwill and Salvation Army stores carry a wide array of items like clothing, shoes, boots, bedding, used appliances, and the like, and they are in good shape, some almost like new. Dollar stores are usually a collection of disorganized junk, but you can find basic household and personal goods like cosmetics, hand lotions, cleaning supplies, garbage bags, and other items at minimal prices. (And pails!!! I found pails for $1 each and bought a whole armload!)

Finally, you can find the MOST amazing treasures at rummage sales. For instance, at a neighborhood rummage sale, I recently bought two excellent revolving fans for $3 each that would have cost me $40 each in a store. Never pass one by. Tuck a few extra dollars of cash in your wallet or purse to pay for the items because they don't take American Express.

TIP:
You will also benefit from taking a walking tour of the Goodwill, Salvation Army, or local dollar store. Take a little time and just walk around making mental notes. Obviously, if you see something on your list, you should get it then.

Household Supplies

You will want to look around your home to assemble a complete list of what you use on a daily basis, but there are some basic supplies everyone should have:

☑ A lot of sturdy garbage bags

TIP:
Here is where you can make up for your previously shabby attitude about the importance of Saving the Earth From Global Warming . . . er, Global Cooling . . . um, Climate Change because you take your groceries and other purchases home in . . . gasp! Plastic bags! (Where is your conscience? Why do you hate the Earth?) Save them— especially the big ones. They're free and you are recycling. You are now officially a "Friend of the Earth." Congratulations!!

☑ A lot of sandwich bags, gallon bags, tin foil, etc. A lot of them, as you can't make a plastic bag when they are gone.

☑ Cleaning products of all types

☑ Hand dishwashing and dishwasher detergents (including liquid dish soap)

☑ Sponges and other cleaning equipment

☑ Paper towels

☑ Bathroom cleaning supplies: toilet bowl cleaner, etc.

☑ Latex gloves

☑ Pest control: RAID or any other pest control items for spiders, wasps, cockroaches, etc.

☑ A clock that runs on batteries and has an alarm

☑ Paper plates, bowls, cups, and cutlery

☑ A non-electric vacuum. Walmart carries the Bissell hand sweeper for about $25.

☑ An old-fashioned percolator to make coffee on the stove, and a small coffee grinder if you have stocked whole coffee beans instead of ground coffee.

☑ A manual can opener

Personal Hygiene Supplies

Take a quick look under your bathroom sink.

☑ Toilet paper

☑ Hand soap (bars of soap can be used as barter, so stock up)

TIP:
A soap-making business might not be a bad idea in the FEND or OTG world. You might want to check into how to make soap now, while you still can.

☑ Women's needs: tampons or sanitary napkins

☑ Hand lotions

☑ Shampoos and conditioners

☑ Razors

☑ Diapers and baby care supplies. You may want to buy some cloth diapers, in addition to stocks of disposable diapers, as you will eventually run out of the disposable ones if the emergency is long enough.

☑ An extra pair of eyeglasses or contacts

Clothing Needs

☑ A sewing machine and sewing supplies such as needles, thread, straight and safety pins, etc. You should buy a little battery-powered sewing machine as well. It's mostly for mending and sewing simple things, but it may come in handy if there is no power.

☑ Get a stock of underwear and socks.

☑ Extra clothing of the type that may be worn a great deal (and worn out) in a FEND or OTG situation: jeans, sweat pants, heavy pullovers (if the climate requires), etc.

☑ Extra pairs of SHOES and BOOTS!!! These are not shoes for work, but walking shoes, sneakers, and sturdy boots. They will wear out fast if you are walking a lot more. Where will you be then? It's not like you can make shoes and boots at home.

Home Repair Supplies

You may find that you have to repair things in your home or build other items in a long-term situation. You should have:

☑ A basic tool kit that contains a hammer, drill, hand saw, pliers, screw drivers, wrenches, etc. Don't forget a good supply of different sizes of nails and screws.

☑ String, rope, and wire

☑ Duct tape or packing tape (and tape gun)

PREPPER RULE #3: You can never have too much duct tape!

☑ A pair of safety glasses

☑ A manual knife sharpener

☑ Super glue (a lot of it) and regular glue for fixing shoes and other items around the house

☑ Oil such as 10W40 (or similar)

☑ Electrician's tapeVelcro by the roll

☑ A good sharp knife and a knife sharpening kit

☑ Utility knives and replacement blades

☑ Several sturdy tarps of various sizes

☑ Big rolls of plastic sheeting

☑ Pails—lots and lots of pails or containers.

☑ A large rolling garbage or leaf container. This can be used for many things, such as collecting and storing rainwater.

Laundry

Have you thought how you will wash clothing if your washer and dryer aren't going to be working for awhile? You will need:

☑ A large sturdy pot for washing clothes

☑ Laundry detergent

☑ Clothes pins and a laundry line

☑ Utility gloves

Sanitation

I doubt many of us have given much consideration to what we would do if we could not use our toilets. No time like the present to start.

☑ You can get a big plastic pail or bucket with a lid that SEALS TIGHTLY. Purchase a toilet seat from the home improvement store to put on top of the bucket. Also get a LOT of sturdy garbage bags. Line the pail or bucket with a garbage bag, lap it over the top, put the toilet seat on it when needed and seal it up again when you are finished. The garbage bags should be treated with chemicals, if possible, firmly tied or taped shut, and put outside away from the house until garbage pickup returns.

☑ You can also purchase a bucket-style emergency toilet, or even a folding toilet. You can see these at: www.quakekare.com. Chemicals such as those used in airplane, bus, and RV toilets are also available at Internet sites such as www.pacificrvparts.com.

Using the Forms

☑ Set up a **Shopping List** for household and personal hygiene supplies (Appendix B).

☑ You may wish to set up separate lists for items you will be buying locally and items you will be getting from the Internet.

☑ After you have purchased the items, erase them from the **Shopping List** and transfer them to the **Inventory Form** (Appendix C.)

SECTION 8.1: HOUSEHOLD 3-5-7 TRACK

Goal: To get through 3-to-7 days with a minimum of inconvenience and to be able to make some emergency repairs on your home.

You should have paper plates and plastic cutlery, as well as a manual can opener. A percolator for making coffee over a grill may be useful as well.

In the 3-5-7 track, household, personal hygiene, clothing, and laundry supplies are not really an issue. However, you may need some home repair tools and there may possibly be sanitation issues.

Home Repair Supplies

You should have a good basic tool box before an emergency. In the 3-5-7 track, it will help you with minor home repairs to make your home livable as you await the insurance man and the construction company.

It wouldn't be a bad idea to have:

- ☑ Pest control products such as RAID, etc.
- ☑ Rolls of plastic sheeting
- ☑ A few sturdy tarps of various sizes
- ☑ Duct tape, wire, rope, string, etc.

Sanitation and Garbage Management

If you are concerned about losing the use of your bathroom for any period of time, purchase one of the emergency toilets listed in the General Information section, or the supplies for a homemade equivalent.

That's all for 3-5-7!

SECTION 8.2: HOUSEHOLD FEND TRACK

Goal: To be able to offset rising costs or scarcities of household, clothing, and personal hygiene items.

In the FEND track, you will want to lay in supplies of items that may be hard to get, replace, or make in the future. Focus your immediate attention on the clothing, shoes, sewing supplies, home repair, sanitation, and laundry categories. You can acquire other, less critical, items (such as cleaning supplies) later.

Household Supplies

Be sure that you have a lot of garbage bags. These products are petroleum-based in their manufacture, and if gas and oil go sky high, they will get very expensive and may become unavailable. It may seem like a little thing, but what will you put your garbage in? What will you use in your emergency toilet? Remember, save your plastic shopping bags.

If budget is an issue, you can wait on the cleaning supplies and other items, or watch for sales or browse through the direct-buy stores for really good deals.

Personal Hygiene

Buy a lot of toilet paper. You should also get any personal products you must have, such as tampons or sanitary napkins. Don't forget the baby's diapers and other infant care supplies. Finally, stock up on shampoos and conditioners, and other personal hygiene items as well.

TIP:
If possible buy extra soap in bar form as it will make an excellent bartering item.

Clothing Needs

Start with acquiring underwear, socks, shoes, boots, and any basic clothing items that, once worn out, cannot be replaced. Remember that Goodwill and Salvation Army stores are excellent sources if money is tight.

Home Repair Supplies

You should already have a basic tool kit, but you may wish to deepen and expand it with more useful items in more quantities.

> **TIP:**
> You should take a walking tour of Lowe's, Home Depot, or a good local hardware store such as Ace Hardware. Spend a little time and just look at everything. I can spend hours in Ace Hardware and, at least in my area, they often offer sales on gloves, socks, cosmetics, and over-the-counter medicines, as well as other good stuff while they last. Make friends in your local hardware store.

Laundry

It may be that in FEND you do not have the use of your washer and dryer at times. You should have:

- ☑ A large, sturdy pot for washing clothes
- ☑ Laundry detergent
- ☑ Clothes pins
- ☑ Laundry line
- ☑ Utility gloves

Sanitation and Garbage Management

Make sure that you have LOTS of garbage bags and an emergency toilet. You may also wish to think about a long-term site for disposing of the garbage bags if it looks like the big green truck might not come for awhile or at irregular intervals. Wherever you put it should be away from your home, preferably buried and lower than any surface water supply you may wish to use. A few bags of lime to sprinkle around the disposal area may be a good idea. You can get bags of lime at your local hardware store or home repair store.

> **TIP:**
> Garbage bags, sandwich bags, etc. take up a lot of room in boxes. You can take them out and store them in a box or plastic bins and save a lot of room, as well as have them all in the same place.

That s it!!! You're done with the FEND track.

SECTION 8.3: HOUSEHOLD OTG TRACK

Goal: To be able to live Off The Grid for a long period of time and able to take care of yourself, your family, and home.

The OTG track is just FEND made deeper and wider—and maybe forever. The longer you can make your beefed up FEND supplies last, the better off you will be before you have to revert to an 18th century lifestyle.

TIP:

Matthew Stein's book, *When Technology Fails*, has an enormous amount of information in it regarding practical living at the OTG level. That's just another good reason to buy it. Holly Drennan Deyo's *Dare To Prepare!* has chapters on how to make soap, candles and your own cleaning supplies, and is, overall, a virtual bible for OTG life.

TRANSPORTATION

*A city that outdistances man's walking powers is
a trap for man.*

~ Arnold J. Toynbee ~

Chapter 9

Hurricane Ike plowed through the Gulf of Mexico and piled into Texas in September 2008. Some of the oil refineries were damaged, and it took several weeks to make the repairs and to start everything up again.

It took a few days for the effects to hit. First, fuel prices rose sharply. Actually, they were changing the numbers on the signs before Ike even arrived, but every day after it hit, gas cost twenty cents more than the day before. Soon the price didn't matter very much because gas wasn't available at all.

First, I noticed that my favorite gas station would run out of fuel for a few days, and then it would have some again. Then it would close again. One week later, about half of the gas stations were closed and looked like they were going to stay that way. At the open stations, there were lines, but they weren't extremely long yet.

Two weeks later, only one in four stations was open at all, at any time. Some days a closed station would get a shipment, open briefly, and a few hours later, it would be closed again. After two weeks I—and everyone else—was getting really concerned. One day I passed 17 gas stations on both sides of the street on a main road and every single one of them was closed.

Luckily, my tank had been nearly full, and I cut down on any extra travel other than getting to work. But finally, I absolutely had to have gas. I set out to find any station that was open. I didn't even bother with the main roads. I ran the lesser roads for 1-1/2 hours and finally found one station that was open. It was on a corner and had entrances from both streets on which it was fronted. The lines out both entrances were three and four blocks long. I waited, inching forward. Gas station attendants were directing cars, trying to keep people from cutting in or starting fights. Tempers were frayed. You prayed that the pump you'd finally get assigned to would not be just vapors by the time you got there. In the end I got eight gallons and was thrilled. The price was around $5 a gallon but I didn't care. It took about 2-1/2 hours to accomplish and I spent one gallon of gas finding the place.

The situation had gotten to the point that people started following gas tankers around. If a fuel tanker was spotted cruising down the road, there was a line of cars creeping behind it, waiting to see if it got on the highway and left the area, or went to a local station.

After about three weeks, the pipelines started to fill again. The gas stations opened up and by four weeks, we had forgotten the whole thing.

That was just one hurricane that didn't even really break anything significant. It was a dramatic example of what will happen if gas truly becomes scarce or very expensive long term.

What if a war in the Middle East created the same effect, but it lasted for many months or a year?

What if gas shot up to $10 per gallon or more? What if the power grid over a regional area was down for a long period of time and you couldn't get gas at all since electricity is needed to pump it out of the ground from the tank into your car?

How do you get to work? How do you get your children to school? What errands are necessary? Who will spend half a day each week trying to find gas at any cost?

No matter how you cut it, at least for the time being, your way of life has changed. If it is a permanent condition, then life as you know it is over.

General Information

Many of the readers of this guide probably live in a sprawling urban community where cars aren't a luxury—they are vital to life.

You should think of transportation as an upside-down triangle.

LEVEL 1: TOTAL MOBILITY

LEVEL 2: IMPAIRED MOBILITY
DUE TO COST OR SCARCITY:
SOME ALTERNATIVES
TO CARS

LEVEL 3:
FOOT
POWER

As of today we enjoy total mobility. We can go anywhere, anytime, at reasonable cost. The cost of fuel may go up at times and we grumble, but we adjust our budgets or our lifestyle slightly and go on.

However, if something happens to the gas supply—if it is rationed, scarce (as after Hurricane Ike), or too expensive for most budgets—then your life style changes, maybe dramatically.

Each level down reduces your ability to move around exponentially, until at last, you are left with your feet. Your world becomes as far as you can walk or pedal.

There are really only two broad things that might happen, which can be planned for:

☑ Gas is so expensive or scarce that you have to change your lifestyle. There is no more TOTAL MOBILITY, but neither are you walking—yet.

☑ Something happens to your car itself (i.e., it is electronically fried in an EMP attack) or fuel simply dries up and becomes unavailable. NOW you are really mobility impaired. In fact, the only places you can go are where your feet—in good sturdy shoes or on pedals—can take you.

There are a few things you can do, but this is going to be a tough system to have to greatly curtail or do without. There are no easy answers.

SECTION 9.1:
TRANSPORTATION 3-5-7 TRACK

Goal: To keep your car filled up with gas so that in an emergency you can concentrate on other important issues, like retrieving family or if you need to evacuate.

There are two things you can do to help yourself in a 3-5-7 event:

☑ The most important thing you can do is to get in the habit of not letting your gas tank get below half a tank. If you get accustomed to keeping your car(s) fueled up, in an emergency you can focus on retrieving your family and, in the event of an evacuation, spend your time loading your car and getting away from the area before millions of others are doing the same thing. You can delay getting gasoline until you are away from populated areas where gas lines may be non-existent or shorter.

☑ Keep some gas on hand in containers that meet government safety standards. Since gasoline deteriorates over time, you should treat it with Sta-Bil, which is available at any hardware store, and which extends its lifetime. After one year, you should take the gas to a car repair facility to be recycled. DO NOT empty it out into the environment. Then refresh your supplies. Store it in a cool, dry place in a proper container, preferably away from the house. You should keep at least five gallons on hand. You should know and follow the local regulations for storing gasoline in or near your home.

That's it!! You're done for 3-5-7.

SECTION 9.2:
TRANSPORTATION FEND TRACK

Goal: To mitigate high gas prices, or rationed or unavailable fuel situations.

In a FEND situation, gasoline may become so expensive that we are forced to limit our travel to only the most necessary. Those who have to travel long distances to work may find that they need to take public transportation when gas reaches a certain price. You should find out about the bus and/or train schedules (if you have a subway system). Where are the stations and bus stops? What are the fares? What are the pertinent bus routes?

In a situation where gas prices are cripplingly high or gas is rationed or unavailable at times, there are a few other options than battling your way to work on crowded trains and buses:

☑ As in 3-5-7, keep a supply of gasoline on hand and rotate it around in case you need it in a critical emergency situation.

 TIP:
Purchase a long length of tubing for siphoning gas in an emergency. You can get it at the hardware store. They will cut the length you wish to buy.

☑ You might want to consider purchasing (before the crisis) a motor scooter, or moped, or similar small motorized vehicle. You can buy a new moped at a local distributor, or used at various sites on the Internet. A used moped may cost as little as $500. Not for nothing do large numbers of Europeans use mopeds instead of cars. Mopeds or scooters get hundreds of miles on a few gallons of gas and could ease the burden of very local travel. Where I live you do not need to register a moped or get a license. You should check your own local regulations and follow them. You should also purchase proper safety equipment such as helmets and reflective lights.

☑ Purchase at least one bicycle and keep it in shape. It wouldn't hurt to use it on a regular basis, even if only for enjoyment on a nice summer evening. We are not talking an expensive racing bike with all the bells and whistles, just a basic three-speed bicycle to get you around the neighborhood, to the grocery store, or on other errands.

You can purchase a used bicycle from sites on the web or at local bike stores, although it is usually cheaper to purchase it from another person looking to sell.

TIP:
You can attach a basket(s) on your bike or purchase a bicycle trailer, which is a small cart that can be attached to the back of the bicycle, for going to the grocery store and other errands. They can be found in department stores such as Target and Walmart in the bicycle section and usually run about $100 or so.

☑ Make sure that you have extra tires, chains, oil and maintenance equipment, and that the bike has proper reflective lights on it.

☑ You will have to depend more on your feet. You should make sure you have several good pairs of comfortable walking shoes. The matter of shoes is treated in full in the Household Section, but having several pairs of good shoes in the FEND and OTG tracks will be <u>one of the most important things</u> you can do for yourself and your family.

TIP:
Buy a wire utility cart with strong and stable wheels. They fold up flat but, when they are expanded, you can carry a sizeable amount of groceries or other items in them. They can be put to many uses. These utility carts are sold in department stores and I have seen them in hardware and home improvement stores as well. They cost about $30.

It's unsatisfactory, given our dependence on cars in our current daily life, but there really isn't much you can do to mitigate fuel issues other than conserve and find other ways to get around cheaply and efficiently.

SECTION 9.3:
TRANSPORTATION OTG TRACK

Goal: To be able to function in a world without cars.

If a terrible disaster occurs, such an EMP attack that burns out everything electronic, then our cars are dead. No car built after the mid-1970s is immune from some form of computer control. If the computers are fried, your car just became a metal and plastic sculpture. You might as well siphon the gas out of it because that's about all that's left of it you can use.

TIP:
A small wagon or collapsible grocery or utility cart might be useful for hauling items like food and water for a short distance. You can find them on the Internet at outlets like http://www.stacksandstacks.com/. They cost about $40.

All you have left are your feet, a bicycle in an urban area, and possibly horses in a rural area. The only "good news" is that we don't have all that many places left to go any more.

BUILDING A GO-BAG

Can you hear me? Can you hear me running?

~ Mike and the Mechanics ~
Silent Running

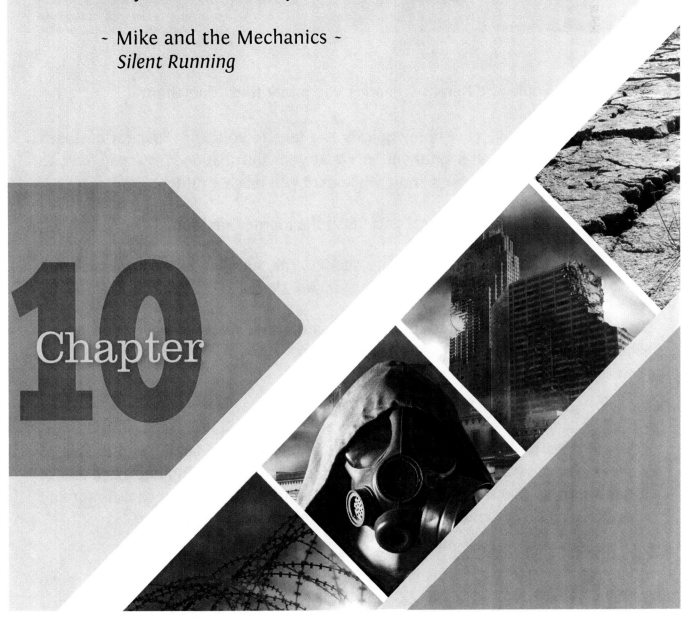

Chapter

10

BUILDING A GO-BAG

Goal: To build a Go-Bag for each member of your family in case you must leave your home quickly, you need to get from one place to another on foot, or to tide you over in a shelter.

Your Go-Bag is not a backpack for surviving in the wilderness. If you are concerned about the possibility of living in the outdoors for a long period and are not an experienced hiker, climber, or camper, you should seek other sources for information on how to build a survival kit for this purpose and to learn about the necessary skills.

TIP:
Matt Stein's book, *When Technology Fails*, is a good starting source for this type of information.

There are a couple of different scenarios you might find yourself in:

☑ Having to leave your home quickly and take to your car. Your car becomes your mobile shelter until you arrive at your destination. You may have to eat and sleep in it for a short while until you reach a refuge.

☑ You have to leave your car and finish the journey on foot.

☑ You are going to a community shelter. The supplies in the backpack will sustain you for the length of time you are there.

There aren't really three tracks here. You are either ready to go or you aren't, whether the emergency lasts one day or longer.

Backpacks

You will need to build a Go-Bag for each member of your family who is able to walk and/or carry any kind of weight. Do not purchase a rolling backpack unless it has straps so that it can also be worn on the back. If you have to walk for any distance, you do not know what ground conditions will be like.

A small child's Go-Bag should contain only a change of clothing, with some room allowed for special items that will comfort them such as a favorite stuffed toy or a game to give them something to do.

The adults' Go-Bags do not need to be expensive hiking backpacks which are designed to allow you to carry your life support systems on your back for an extended period of time. Camping and hiking stores, and websites offer a bewildering array of backpacks that often have every bell and whistle favored by aficionados and hardcore hikers. It's truly amazing how complex such a backpack can be with zippers, pockets, clips, rain protection, perfect balance, padding, and fit issues, all of which are critical for long treks in the woods, but are not necessary for a Go-Bag.

Your Go-Bag should have a place to hook a water bottle and some outside pockets and places to tuck things, be comfortable to wear and, when fully loaded, not so large or heavy that the user is overburdened if he has to walk more than a few miles. You can get a perfectly reasonable backpack for this purpose at Walmart (or most department stores) for much less money (around $40 to $60). I got mine at Walmart and it has lots of pockets and can be converted into a duffle bag.

If necessary, some provision should be made for one of the adults to carry an infant without using their arms, if using a stroller becomes impossible.

You should keep the Go-Bag ready with the exception of adding, just before you leave, a change of clothing (which will vary depending on the climate and season). Every member of the family must have a pair of comfortable walking shoes (or boots) and they should be kept in the backpack at all times. Be sure you break them in before storing them away in the Go-Bag.

Evacuation

Almost every day you hear about some residential neighborhood or large area being evacuated due to wildfires, industrial accidents, hurricanes, or any number of other disasters. In a large-scale unexpected evacuation, the roads will be clogged within an hour or two, so time is of the essence. If you must go, then be one of the first. You should have detailed local and regional maps in the car, and have plotted at least one way out of town (preferably two or three) via roads that will be less crowded. Being one of the first on the road will give you the first pick of lodgings, gas and other needs as you go.

If you are going to a shelter or will be in the car for some time (and you should plan that the journey will take much longer than you anticipate), you will want to pack the following things in the car. You should have prepared a list beforehand so that the items can be checked off as they are loaded.

☑ You should have your important documents all in one place, such as a fireproof safe. Throw the whole safe into the car. In addition, make copies of some of your more important documents, put them in a plastic bag, and stow them in a security travel pouch on your person. These may include your mortgage, insurance papers, birth certificates, social security card, critical medical information, important prescriptions, etc.

TIP:

Ladies, don't take your purse. Empty the essential items out and leave them home. Take only your wallet, credit cards, cell phone, etc. You should purchase a money or security belt used by travelers for hiding valuables and cash under your clothing. They are very common. You can find them at department stores in the travel section or on the Internet. A security belt cost about $20. It might be wise to buy one for every adult in the family and split up the valuables between them.

☑ Make sure you have your cash, credit cards, and any other financial resources or valuables you are unwilling to abandon. Put them in the security travel pouch you wear on your person.

☑ Make sure everyone has their cell phones. Bring the charger as well. You should also add a solar charger in case there is no electricity. (See the "Communications" chapter for ordering information.)

☑ Blankets and pillows or bedrolls.

☑ As many cases of bottled water as your family will need for several days. (You can also purchase pouches of water than can be stored more easily in your backpack.)

☑ Anything that is needed for your pet(s): food, leash, bowls, etc. If you are really organized, you can include their vaccination records in your important records.

☑ Prescription medicines or anything else needed for people with special requirements.

☑ Anything needed for an infant: diapers, food, blankets, clothing, stroller, etc.

☑ A stock of emergency freeze-dried food which can be loaded in the car and, if necessary, redistributed among the backpacks.

TIP:
At the very least, freeze-dried food should be considered for your Go-Bag or for keeping in your car in case of evacuation. The packages that will get you through three days to a week are reasonably priced. For instance, Solutions From Science offers a grab-and-go emergency food supply with 84 servings of food in one bucket that can feed two adults and four children for six days. It includes a nice range of entrees, soups, and breakfast cereals. It costs $179 and you get a nice bucket too! Remember: You can never have too many buckets! You can read about and order it at http://www.foodshortagesolutions.com.

☑ A can of gas and some oil.

Besides climate appropriate clothing the backpacks should contain the following, distributed among them:

☑ A first-aid kit and first-aid book. It wouldn't hurt to carry a few extra roll bandages and a bottle of pain reliever.

☑ A Steri-Pen, water purification pills, filter,or similar water treatment item

☑ A pair of good walking shoes or boots (for each person) and several pairs of socks

☑ Underwear and other personal garments or products

☑ Extra eye glasses or contacts

☑ A Swiss-type knife with a few basic attachments such as a screwdriver, scissors, knife, etc.

☑ A roll of duct tape, a roll of string, and a length of rope

☑ A rain poncho

- ☑ Laundry and dishwashing soap

- ☑ Toilet paper and wet wipes

- ☑ Several flashlights (with extra batteries), and Glo-sticks

- ☑ A small battery-powered lantern (with extra batteries)

- ☑ Cigarette lighters (even if you don't smoke) and some matches

- ☑ A small portable radio (that gets a weather channel) with extra batteries

- ☑ Basic toiletries as required for each person: toothbrush, toothpaste, hairbrush, comb, tissues, female needs, soap, razors, extra eyeglasses, shampoo, hand lotion, mirror, etc.

- ☑ An emergency blanket

- ☑ A compass and a whistle

- ☑ Sewing kit with extra thread

- ☑ A medium-sized towel and washcloth

- ☑ A cup, bowl, and cutlery for each person

- ☑ Cooking gear: a small pot, a skillet with knives, forks and spoons for preparing and serving food. You only need one set of these items.

- ☑ Large garbage bags

- ☑ Face masks (several for each person)

- ☑ A pair of utility gloves

- ☑ Food treats and snacks

- ☑ A deck of cards or light portable computer game, reading materials, puzzle book, etc. for entertainment

- ☑ Depending on the climate or time of year, don't forget a hat, sunglasses and sun block, or similar items for the winter time

- ☑ Paper and pencil or pen

☑ A can opener (unless there is one on your Swiss-type knife)

☑ Everyone's cell phones

☑ Laptop computer

Do not fill every backpack completely. If you need to leave the car and walk, you will have to tuck water, food, and other items in the car into what room is left in the backpacks.

Preparing a list of items to collect quickly is crucial. It would be a shame to idle in long lines on the highway, and have slogged twenty miles in three hours, only to find that Johnny forgot his asthma inhaler and someone left the food behind. And don't forget the cat or dog.

Carry a firearm on your person only if you have a carry permit. Any other firearms should be stored properly in the vehicle according to the rules of your state or locality.

If you need to evacuate but have a few minutes to get out, divide up the tasks. Send someone to gas up the vehicles(s) while the children collect appropriate clothing for themselves. Gather the items on your list and check them off. Pack them up, check your list again, and then get out.

Alternative to Packing Your Own Go-Bag

An alternative to packing your own Go-Bag is the Evac Pack: The Ultimate Survival Kit for Emergency Evacuations. There are two sizes: a rolling duffle bag or a backpack.

☑ The backpack contains a flashlight, water proof matches, two Mylar sleeping bags, work gloves, a small first-aid kit, a water-filtration bottle, portable stove, plates and utensils, and 44 servings of freeze-dried food.

☑ The rolling duffle bag contains the same items, but also includes a two-person tent, ponchos, dust masks, rope, and an emergency candle.

You can find both versions of the Evac Pack at www.myevacpack.com. If one adult carried this core pack, then personal items such as clothing could be spread out across all the other packs. The backpack costs $179 and the rolling duffle bag costs $239.

Setting Up Your Own Go-Bag

Without question, building your own Go-Bag is time consuming, making investing in one of the prepared evacuation bags described above very sensible. You have to buy all the items in the necessary quantities, assemble them, distribute them among the various backpacks, and finally, pack them artfully for easy access. Batteries will have to be collected for items that require them. Personal hygiene items and general items (such as laundry soap) will need to be assembled and prepared. It took me almost a day to get everything together and packed—and that was just one Go-Bag.

The adults' and older children's Go-Bags should contain the heavier items such as food, water, water-filtering equipment, cooking equipment, radios, as well as their own personal items (toothbrushes, toilet paper, etc.) The adults should also carry the money, credit cards, and important papers. Older children should carry the lighter items, and even the smallest child should have a small Go-Bag for their clothes, a little food and water, and a comfort toy. Letting a small child carry some things in their little pink Miss Kitty backpack (or whatever the current rage is) will also help them feel included and useful.

You can't just shove everything in either. When you need your toothbrush and toothpaste, you do not want to have to unpack the entire backpack to get to it. This is where using the pockets and outside compartments will come in handy for items you need to get to quickly and often.

If possible try to get your family involved in the packing. The children should start thinking about the ONE or TWO (at most) compact and portable items they can bring with them. Quarrels and tears about why your children can't bring most of their room with them when you need to get out of your home in one half hour need to be avoided. Then have everyone try them on. You will be surprised at how heavy they are. A short walk (about one mile) with them around the block or on a local hiking trail in a park should impress the children (and yourself) that "less is more" in this situation.

Storing Your Go-Bags

Keep one comprehensive Go-Bag in the car, along with basic food and water at all times. Store the others in your home, mostly assembled except for the last items, which should take only minutes to assemble.

Using the Forms

☑ Set up a **Shopping List** for items you are purchasing for your Go-Bag(s) (Appendix B).

☑ You may wish to set up separate lists for items you will be buying locally and items you will be getting from the Internet.

☑ After you have purchased the items, erase them from the **Shopping List** and transfer them to the **Inventory Form** (Appendix C.)

☑ Record all the tasks and items you want to take with you on the **Evacuation List** (Appendix D) and keep it somewhere you can find it fast.

BARTER

Their manner of trading is for copper, beads, and such like, for which they give such commodities as they have, as skins, fowl, fish, flesh, and their country corn. But their victuals are their chiefest riches.

~ Capt. John Smith ~
1580 - 1631

Chapter

11

BARTER

If we end up in an OTG world for an extended period of time, there are certain items which will be priceless in the "New World." Among these are:

- ☑ Coffee
- ☑ Soap
- ☑ Salt
- ☑ Pepper
- ☑ Sugar
- ☑ Alcohol
- ☑ Cigarettes
- ☑ Candles
- ☑ Bleach (for purifying water)
- ☑ Ammunition
- ☑ Toilet paper
- ☑ Pain relievers

As you purchase your food stocks, if possible, set aside some of the items above in more quantities than you feel you need for your immediate family needs. For the food stuffs, the grocery store is NOT the place to do this, however. You need to find a direct-buy outlet or farmers market that sells to restaurants or the food industry. They will carry large bags of items like salt and sugar at the best price possible.

And yes, you should consider buying cigarettes—especially if you DON'T smoke (since you won't smoke up your stock in desperation!!!!) Search the web using "discount cigarettes" and you can usually find a source that sells them for half the cost of gas stations and other stores. You might also check for a physical outlet in your area so you do not have to buy online. A good source is www. discountcigarettesmall.com, but there are many others.

Store any of this stuff you buy for barter carefully and securely because it may be your "income" in the future. Anyone who runs a business involving any of these items—or anything that might have any value in the New World—should immediately sequester them in a secure hiding place at the first clear sign of a long-term emergency.

PETS

Animals are such agreeable friends - they ask no questions, they pass no criticisms.

- George Eliot -

12

Chapter

PETS

Don't forget the other members of your family.

Evacuation

Be sure that you have proper carriers, cages, bedding, litter, litter boxes, collar (with pet's ID, name, address, rabies tag and license), water bottles, bowls, leashes, medicines, food for at least one week, vaccination records, waste disposal (plastic garbage bags), grooming supplies, a toy, and any other items necessary to transport and control your pet, ready to go. You should have a recent photo of your pet. You might want to pack them their own small Go-Bag so it can be grabbed up quickly in an emergency.

And don't forget your friend as you rush out the door.

Longer-Term Situations

For longer periods of time, be sure you have stored up a good supply of food, bedding, litter, and anything else your pet uses regularly.

Some pet stores can be pretty expensive, so check at places like Walmart or other department stores for some low cost foods and other items in large sizes. Dried food would be best, as canned food will suffer the same fate as people food—it has to be rotated out and used after a period of time.

Using the Forms

☑ Set up a **Shopping List** for items you are purchasing for your pets (Appendix B).

☑ After you have purchased the items, erase them from the **Shopping List** and transfer them to the **Inventory Form** (Appendix C.)

GARDENING

God made rainy days so gardeners could get the housework done.

- Author Unknown -

Chapter

13

GARDENING

This is not a chapter on HOW to garden. It is a basic list of items you will need if you want to begin a small garden of your own.

Basic Tools

☑ Shovels, hoes, rakes, hedge clippers, and a hatchet

☑ Hand-gardening tools

☑ Stakes and poles, large balls of string, twine, etc.

☑ Gloves (several pairs)

☑ Boots and a hat

TIP:
I can't stress highly enough getting proper footwear for slogging around in the dirt. I bought a bright blue pair of rubber boots at Target for what I thought was a little bit too much money. However, those boots have turned out to be one of my absolutely best buys ever. Not only can I slog around in any kind of soil conditions and remain perfectly dry, but they also protect my feet from bugs and animal bites. I wear them when I stomp around the woods cutting wood. Since they are rubber, they can be rinsed off and tipped over to dry. You should definitely get a good pair of boots.

You may also need "tomato towers," but which can be used to guide the growth of any plant. You can also consider purchasing wildlife or garden netting which can be used to protect against birds and animals, or for directing climbing or spreading plants into desired areas. This mesh is available in rolls or square sheets from most garden centers and home improvement stores, and is reusable and inexpensive.

Any of these things will be available for a few dollars at a garden center or home improvement store. You may also wish to purchase:

☑ A soil testing kit

☑ A water meter to measure rainfall

☑ An outdoor thermometer

☑ Hoses and hose heads

☑ Seed starter supplies or kits for beginning your garden indoors

☑ And PAILS!!! Don't forget pails!! They are an absolute necessity.

Seeds and Planting Accessories

You can buy your own seeds. If you do, you should try not to buy hybrid seeds as they will not reproduce next year if you save some of them for seed. Many seed packets boast that they are "Organic," but that designation only means that they were grown without pesticides. A hybrid can be grown organically but still not reproduce next year.

What you want are "heirloom" seeds, that is, seeds from plants that have been carefully grown, untampered with, and uncrossed with other species for years—even centuries. Heirloom seeds will not only provide you with food, but will provide the seeds for your next year's garden. These seeds are not as easy to find.

TIP:
If you buy your own seeds, you will need to seal them with your Seal-A-Meal and store them in a cool dry place.

A very good choice for starting a garden is:

☑ <u>The Survival Seed Bank.</u> The seeds in this bank are all "heirloom" seeds and there are enough to plant a full acre. Each seed pack is individually wrapped for maximum shelf life. They are dried precisely, then sealed in a special foil packet with a desiccant designed to keep the seeds fresh for 20 years at 70 degrees. Freezing your seed bank will increase its shelf life by five times. It all comes in an indestructible plastic tube in which the seeds can be stored easily. Each bank contains $500 worth of heirloom seeds from a retailer. The seeds include: Jacob's Cattle Bean; Black Valentine Bean, Stringless; Bountiful Bean; Cylindra Beet; Early Jersey Wakefield Cabbage; Stowell's Evergreen Corn; Reid's Yellow Dent Corn; White Wonder Cucumber; Yellow of Parma Onion; Giant Nobel Spinach; Scarlet Nantez Carrot; Red Salad Bowl Lettuce; Susan's Red Bibb Lettuce; Schoon's Hard Shell Melon; Green Arrow Pea, Fordhook Giant Chard; Druzba Tomato; Golden Treasure Pepper; Jimmy Nardello's Pepper; French Breakfast Radish; Pink Banana Squash; and Rossa Bianca Eggplant. This seed bank costs only $150. You can read about it and order it at www.survivalseedbank.com.

☑ In conjunction with the Survival Seed Bank, you can also purchase a beginning stock of herb seeds in the form of the Survival Herb Bank: Herbal Remedies Crisis Garden so you can grow your own herbs for medicines. It contains many common herb seeds including: catnip, arnica, feverfew, boneset, valerian, black cohosh, Echinacea, Florence fennel, evening primrose, calendula, chicory, comfrey, chamomile, lavender, cayenne, yarrow, rosemary, lemon balm, hyssop, and marshmallow. The herb bank costs about $100 plus shipping. You may read about it and order it at http://www.survivalherbbank.com/. You also get a free companion e-book called *How To Grow Your Own Herbs for Survival Remedies*.

☑ Finally, you should consider purchasing ProtoGrow™, which is a plant "superfood" that eliminates the need for fertilizer. It's made of sea nutrients and results in an extended production season, more growth, and more mineral uptake. You may read about this fertilizer at www.growlikecrazy. com. It costs $30.

TIP:
I found a small plastic seed sower in the garden section of my local department store that I have found very useful. You take the clear top off, put the seeds inside and move the dial until it matches the size of the seed you wish to sow. In this way you can control the number and density of the seeds you sow in your rows with a lot more precision than trying to sprinkle them by hand.

Cultivator

You will also need cultivation equipment. If possible, you should purchase a gas-powered cultivator for preparing the ground. Do NOT buy an electrically-powered cultivator. It is best to buy a cultivator at the end of the gardening season because then they are on sale. There are many different types, some with different attachments. A gas-powered cultivator should cost between $200 and $300.

There are manual cultivators as well, which you can get at home improvement and gardening stores. These include a version of the blades of a powered cultivator for turning over the earth and breaking it up. There is also a tool that you drive into the ground with your foot and then turn by hand to break up the earth. Both are very hard work to use, especially on unbroken or only lightly turned ground, but you will have them in the event there is no gas to be found anywhere.

A Garden Utility Cart

After the boots, the most magnificent purchase I have yet to make is a wonderful green collapsible canvas wagon. It has sturdy wheels, a strong handle, and a canvas cover for when it is folded up. I would not be able to manhandle around the sacks of mulch, compost, piles of weeds, and everything else without it. It is truly amazing. It cost me $80 and it was a fantastic buy.

There are many of these utility or garden carts in all styles and shapes. A search of the web under "gardening carts" will produce a wide variety for you to choose from. They are also available at gardening centers and home improvement stores. The Red Folding Wagon at http://www.nextag.com/Red-Folding-Wagon-680204926/prices-html?nxtg=6d7a0a28050e-23FF7A29574398E7 is an example.

Finally, if you think gardening is drifting around with a basket over your arm and a wide-brimmed hat on, snipping delicately at well-behaved and neat plants, you are mistaken. It's harder work than you realize if you have never done it. You have to prepare the ground, drag big sacks of dirt and compost and mulch, hoe, weed, sow your seeds, nurture them into life, weed some more, water, weed some more, chase pests and animals away, prune and thin, water, and weed some more. After you pick your food you have to clean it. THEN you eat it. It's not instant, but it is very satisfying.

You will get very dirty and sweaty, and sometimes very hot. Wear a hat, cover exposed skin, pace yourself, drink a lot of fluids, and do your gardening work early in the morning. You should apply insect repellant spray liberally and wear gloves, especially when you weed.

You should invest in several good gardening handbooks. In this matter you would benefit from going to the actual book store and looking through them to find the ones that will be of the most use to you. You can also order them from Amazon.

Ultimately, gardening is a truly amazing and satisfying thing for a city dweller to do. It's almost mystical to watch the seeds sprout and grow into food. For the first time you realize where all that food in the supermarket comes from, and how much effort and knowledge is put into growing it and getting it to you. After all the hard work is done, it is fun to pick your food, clean it and eat it fresh. There is nothing like it. It's a real accomplishment based on hard work—and it could prove very important in a FEND or OTG world.

Using the Forms

☑ Set up a **Shopping List** for items you are purchasing for gardening (Appendix B).

☑ After you have purchased the items, erase them from the **Shopping List** and transfer them to the **Inventory Form** (Appendix C.)

WHAT DO I DO NOW?
PUTTING IT ALL TOGETHER

Some are so perfectly prepared for the expected that they are
defeated by the unexpected.

- Rabbi Schraga Silverstein

If you have read this far, you know now that I was not exaggerating when I told you that this project was going to take commitment, time, and money. Many of you may be intimidated by the job ahead at this point and still don't know how (or are reluctant) to start—and I don't blame you. Honestly, if I had known ahead of time the scope and extent of what I started out to do nearly two years ago, like the Turkey in the fable at the beginning of the book, I might have decided to use my money to take a series of vacations instead so that I would at least have been tanned and rested when the apocalypse came.

You may find it interesting how I came to devote all this energy and time to this project. I didn't have a single moment of enlightenment. Rather, I came to realize that I needed to prepare by a gradual process. The financial crisis at the end of 2007 seriously frightened me, and started me thinking about the very real possibility of losing everything and what I could do to hedge against it. (The answer? Nothing, really.) Then we elected a new president who, from the first minute, ignored economic realities and continued digging away at the hole we were in with heavy equipment at full speed. I realized that there was a big wall looming in our future, and we were driving straight toward it at full speed. There was no doubt in my mind any longer that, without a miracle, this was all going to come to a bad end—the only questions were "When?" and "Do I have time to get ready?"

Then something more personally impactful happened: I read a book. The book was William Forstchen's *One Second After*. That book changed my life. It stunned me, literally, and raised my desire to prepare to an urgent level. One last event occurred that cemented my commitment to my new direction: I moved. I had been saving for a long time to move, and had my heart set upon leaving the big city I lived in and burying myself in the countryside beside the ocean. It was a beacon that drove me on to sacrifice and save, to plan and work. I wanted it so badly, I could taste it. The financial crash ended that dream. I took it hard, as I had nurtured my dream for nearly two years, and then it was over in just a week or two. I experienced real grief for that lost dream. I was going to have to stay in the city where I had work, and settle down to keeping my job at all costs.

After I recovered, I realized that this didn't mean I couldn't maximize my position as best as I could. I found a house that was reasonably distant from major roads out of town, had a woods surrounding it, a stream out back that led to a major river one mile away, had a fenced-in yard with room for garden, a fireplace, storage space, and which, strangest of all, I reckoned could be secured by blocking off the road. If my real estate agent had known as we turned the corner into the area on that first inspection that I was thinking, *Hmmmm, that street can be closed off from either end and secured...* she would have driven me straight to a mental institution instead of a house viewing. After I moved in, my preparations began in earnest.

Initially, I didn't have any kind of an overview about where I was heading, just a vague aspiration that I wanted to be able to take care of myself if everything crashed around me. I gathered items on a paycheck-by-paycheck basis (and still do), always having to maneuver around a series of financial crises that continue to this day to disrupt my best laid plans. Slowly I built each system without really understanding the big picture. This book is the result of that learning experience, with many wrong turns, backtracking, and poor investments—from which you get to benefit. Trust me, though, when I say that if <u>I can do it, you can too</u>. I had no extraordinary financial resources then—and certainly don't now after this exercise. As I neared the end, I began to see a pattern in what I had done and thought that what I had learned might help others straighten their road. You are reading it now.

For those of you who have real financial resources, you could complete the entire job within one month to six weeks in a burst of serious ordering from the Internet and a series of mop-up trips to local stores.

TIP:

For those of you with really remarkable resources, you may wish to consider converting already-owned property or purchasing additional property in a more isolated area, but within reach of your current residence where you can create a secure retreat and make it the focus of all your preparation. This is especially true for those whose primary property is in the heart of, or in the major suburbs of, a large city. The wisest course of action in a real emergency would be to leave the city entirely at the first hint of trouble. The truth is that if I suddenly won the lottery now, despite all the work I have put in here, I would instantly run for the woods myself.

However, most of us are going to have to organize and prioritize. So, if you still want to do this, here is how to take all this information and begin:

- ☑ Read the manual once to absorb the overall ideas and content, and decide what level of commitment, finances, and time you wish to commit.

- ☑ Decide on the track for which you wish to prepare.

- ☑ Start from the top of the book again. Make copies of the **Shopping List** forms and start filling them in using each chapter as a basis.

- ☑ You should put everything you want to get on the lists, even if you know you can't afford it right now (or maybe even never). But put it on anyway.

- ☑ Keep your compiled lists together in a binder or file so you can find them to review, add to, and update.

- ☑ Prioritize what you want to tackle first in each system. Use a "1" for items that are the most critical and which you must get first; "2" for secondary items, etc. For items that qualify in the "10" category put them on a "When Pigs Fly" list. At least they are there and, if the opportunity happens, you can move swiftly to acquire them.

- ☑ Begin your scouting trips through the supermarket, home improvement store, local hardware store, pharmacy, dollar store, Goodwill or Salvation Army stores, farmers markets, etc. Set aside some time to discover what is in them so that you can conduct your shopping efficiently and cost-effectively.

- ☑ If money and time are issues, focus first on the "Big Four": Water, Food, Medicine and Security, as you begin shopping. You can sweep up items in the other categories as opportunity or budget allows.

- ☑ Be sure to move your items from the **Shopping List** to the **Inventory List** as you go.

- ☑ As you acquire your supplies, follow the storage instructions and hide them.

TIP:

If you cannot afford to buy all the electric gadgets in the FEND track, jump to the OTG track and buy the manual equivalent first. For example, if you want a food dehydrator and budget is an issue, then get a non-electric food dehydrator like the Food Pantrie. That way, in either FEND or OTG, you can dry food no matter what. When budget and time permits, you can go back and fill in the FEND track with an electric food dehydrator. This is what I did.

☑ Be silent about your preparations.

☑ Remember—time may be of the essence.

If your spouse or partner is not sure about whether preparing is important, encourage him to read or listen to *One Second After*. Ask them to look long and hard at their family after they finish it. After that, they'll probably help, not hinder you.

That's really it. The rest is the relentless activity: shopping, inventorying, preserving, and hiding it. Getting discouraged, tired and doubtful is part of the process. Pick up one foot and put it down, pick up the other foot and put it down. Repeat. Repeat. Repeat—over and over again. Sometimes you will feel like you are trying to push mud uphill. Look at your children if you need encouragement. Keep doing that and you will get there. Take a little break . . . okay, that's long enough. Remember that time may be of the essence. Pick up one foot and put it down, pick up the other foot and put it down. Repeat. Repeat. Repeat—over and over again. You can do it. I am living proof.

If, after all, it does come to nothing and the future turns out to be bright, rosy, and prosperous, then that will be truly wonderful. I'll feel a little foolish and then have the Mother Of All Rummage Sales. I will find the floor of my closets once again, and throw out the bottles and plastic sacks with great relief.

But if something terrible does happen, then perhaps you and your family will survive. It will be you and your children who will be the new Founding Fathers and Founding Mothers for our country. Personally, I want to be around to see us at least begin to put this country back on it feet. Remember Abigail Adams—and don't forget the pins!

Good luck, and may God bless you in your journey!!!

BUILDING YOUR SURVIVAL LIBRARY

General Reading - Fiction

William Forstchen, *One Second After* (audio book recommended)

James Howard Kunstler, *World Made by Hand*

General Reading – Non-Fiction/Reference

Holly Drenna Deyo, *Dare to Prepare!* (3rd edition) (2010)

Ben Sherwood, *The Survivors Club: The Secrets and Science that Could Save Your Life*

Matthew Stein, *When Technology Fails: A Manual for Self-Reliance, Sustainability, and Surviving the Long Emergency*

James Wesley, Rawles, *How to Survive the End of the World as We Know It*

The Deyo and Stein books are encyclopedic reference books for living OTG. Both have detailed sections on water, food, shelter, first aid, sanitation and much, much more.

Hiding Stuff

Sam Adams, *Hide Your Guns* at www.hideyourguns.com

Food

Deanna DeLong, *How To Dry Foods: The Most Complete Guide to Drying Foods at Home* (or a similar title)

Carol W. Costenbader, *The Big Book of Preserving the Harvest: 150 Recipes for Freezing, Canning, Drying and Picking Fruits and Vegetables*

Carol Hupping, *Stock Up: The Classic Preserving Guide*

. . . or similar titles possibly including volumes on juicing, growing sprouts and wheatgrass, and making bread.

Food Storage Secrets at www.foodshortageusa.com.

Gone Before You Get There: 77 Items You Must Have... That Instantly Vanish From Store Shelves In A Panic at www.preparedforcrisis.com

Stan Moreland, *Survival Stockpiling* from www.survivalstockpiling.com.

Medical/Dental

American Red Cross First Aid & Safety Handbook

James and Phyllis Balch, *Prescription of Nutritional Healing: A Practical A-Z Reference to Drug-Free Remedies Using Vitamins, Minerals, Herbs & Food Supplements*

Linda B. White and Steven Foster, *The Herbal Drugstore*

Debra St. Claire, *Herbal Preparations and Natural Therapies: Creating and Using a Home Herbal Medicine* Chest (a course on DVDs) at http://www.makeherbalmedicines.com.

Harvard Medical School Family Health Guide (or similar title)

David Werner, *Where There Is No Doctor*

Murray Dickson, *Where There Is No Dentist*

Emergency Herbs: How To Make Your Own "Herbal Antibiotics" ebook at http://www.emergencyherbs.com

Security

Home Defense Tactics at www.HomeDefenseTactics.com.

Sam Adams, *Surviving Martial Law* at www.martiallawsurvival.com

Gardening

Gardening books of your choice from the bookstore.

Other

Sam Adams, *Red Horse: Surviving a Nuclear Blast* at www.dirtybombsurvival.com

Sam Adams, *Pale Horse: Surviving a Biological or Chemical Attack* at www.biowarsurvival.com

APPENDIX A: WORKSHEETS

Ready For Anything: The Ultimate No B.S. Survival Manual For Ordinary People

WORKSHEET 1:
FAMILY WATER CALCULATOR WORKSHEET

NAME OF PERSON OR PET	BASIC DRINKING REQT IN OZ. PER DAY	COOKING WASHING PER DAY	SPECIAL NEEDS PER DAY	TOTAL IN OZ. PER DAY	TOTAL IN GALLONS PER DAY	TOTAL IN PINTS PER DAY
TOTAL PER DAY						

How to use the Water Calculator

1. List the name of your family member or pet.

2. Use the calculator at http://www.csgnetwork.com/humanh2owater.html to calculate the water requirements of each person. For your pet, just make your best guess. If you live in a climate where it is very hot in the summer and cold in the winter, go with the "warm climate." Then you are covered if the emergency happens in hot weather and have a little edge if it happens in cool weather. Round off the ounce figure.

3. Multiply the ounce figure by at least 1.50 to cover light personal washing, cooking and dish washing needs.

4. Add the ounces you figure a special needs person might require above the basic amount. You should multiply by at least 1.50 to cover all possibilities. Don't go below 25 percent though.

5. Add up the total ounces each person needs.

6. Convert the total ounces to gallons by dividing the total ounce figure by 128.

7. If you want a pint figure, divide the gallon figure by 8 to get the number of pint bottles you need.

WORKSHEET 2:
BULK FOOD CALCULATION WORKSHEET

This worksheet is designed to help you figure out how much food your family will need in one year. For example: one average male adult needs:

- ☑ 375 lbs. of grains (whole wheat, pasta, oats, corn, rice, etc.)
- ☑ 60 lbs. of legumes (beans, peas, lentils, soybeans etc.)
- ☑ 60 lbs. of milk, dairy products and eggs
- ☑ 20 lbs. of meat and/or meat substitutions
- ☑ 10 to 30 lbs. of fruits and vegetables
- ☑ 22 lbs. of fats, oils and shortenings (butter, cooking oils, etc.)
- ☑ 20 to 50 lbs. of sprouting seeds and supplies
- ☑ 8 lbs. of salt and another other seasonings

CALCULATING FOOD REQUIREMENTS

	Equivalent Adult Males
1. Multiply the number of adult males in your family by 1.0	--------------------
2. Multiply the number of adult females in your family by .85	--------------------
3. Multiply the number of teenage males x 1.4	--------------------
4. Multiply the number of teenage females x .95	--------------------
5. Multiply the number of male children (7 to 11) by .95	--------------------
6. Multiply the number of female children (7 to 11) by .75	--------------------
7. Multiply the number of children (4 to 6) x 0.6	--------------------
8. Multiply the number of infants (1 to 3) by 0.4	--------------------
TOTAL	--------------------

Take the final total of Equivalent Adult |Males and multiply each of the categories above by that number. That is the amount of grains, legumes, milk, fruit, vegetables, etc. you will need to stock for one year. Divide or multiply the figures for each food category according to the length of time for which you are preparing. This will help you track the amount of your purchases and give you a benchmark for your progress.

(This form is reproduced with the courtesy of Chelsea Green Publishing Company and Matthew Stein, *When Technology Fails: A Manual for Self-Reliance, Sustainability, and Surviving the Long Emergency*. It was itself adapted with permission for James Talmage Stevens, *Making the Best of Basics: Family Preparedness Handbook*.)

APPENDIX B: SHOPPING LISTS

SHOPPING LIST: _____

SHEET #_____

Priority 1,2,3	Item/Source	Amt	Budget Cost	Date Order/ Obtained

How To Use The Shopping Forms:

The forms are generic so fill in the type of **shopping list** on the line provided at the top: i.e., Food (Supermarket), Water Purifying Equipment, Bulk Food, Medical, Dental, Household/Personal Hygiene, etc.

You might want to keep separate forms for shopping in different stores or websites: i.e., one for food from the supermarket, another for bulk or barter foods, and one for supplies. Equipment purchases for water purification, food making, and communications should be kept on a different shopping form as most of these purchases will not come from local stores but from the Internet.

When you have purchased the item, transfer it to a matching **Inventory Form.** (You probably won't need to transfer the equipment purchases as it will be pretty obvious that you have them. Just scratch them off the **Shopping List** until you have everything. However, keeping an **Inventory Form** will be critical for medical, dental, food from the supermarket, etc., otherwise you will completely lose track of what you have and what you need, especially if you mark it and hide it right after your purchase.

On the Shopping Form:

1. Fill in the item name in the second column.

2. Fill in the source for the item. For instance, from a website on the Internet or by vendor.

3. Enter the number of items you wish to buy and mark it in the right hand column.

4. Enter a rough cost so that you know when that item fits into your budget.

5. Then prioritize the items so that, as your budget permits, you can purchase it.

At times you may have to reorganize and re-write your lists as you begin to make big dents in them.

Keep the **Shopping Lists** for the supermarket, drugstores, etc. with you at all times so you can take advantage of sales and promotions. Keep the others in a file or binder so that you can find and update them quickly.

APPENDIX C: INVENTORY FORMS